TECHNIQUE IN FICTION

SECOND EDITION: REVISED AND UPDATED FOR A NEW GENERATION

TECHNIQUE IN FICTION

SECOND EDITION: REVISED AND UPDATED FOR A NEW GENERATION

ROBIE MACAULEY & GEORGE LANNING

St. Martin's Griffin
New York

Library of Congress Cataloging-in-Publication Data

Macauley, Robie.
    Technique in fiction / Robie Macauley & George Lanning.
        p. cm.
    Includes bibliographical references and index.
    ISBN 0-312-05168-9
    1. Fiction—Technique.   I. Lanning, George.   II. Title.
PN3355.M2   1990
808.3—dc20   90-37571
                                                                 CIP

10   9   8   7   6   5   4   3

For John Crowe Ransom

CONTENTS

ACKNOWLEDGMENTS

Our gratitude for wise counsel to Thomas McCormack and George Witte of St. Martin's Press and to Pamela Painter —two editors and one fiction writer of great perception.

INTRODUCTION

People who know little about writing are often pleased to remark, "Nobody can teach you how to write fiction; it isn't an ability that can be taught." If pressed a little further, they will add, "Anyone who has a story to tell can write a novel." Leo Tolstoy must have run into just such people in his time because he once made up another little dialogue. He said if you ask a person if he can play the violin and he answers "Perhaps I can; I've never tried," the answer would seem absurd to everybody. But if you ask, "Can you write [fiction]?" most people would reply quite seriously that they don't know because they haven't tried. Tolstoy's point, of course, is that it takes as much technical learning and skill to write a good novel as it does to play a violin concerto, and no person is born with such skills.

As for teachers of writing, there are any number of fine ones available. Some of their names are Austen, Dickens, Joyce, Tolstoy, Woolf, Flaubert, Hemingway, Faulkner. And Updike, Bellow, Singer, Trevor, Lessing, Bowen, Gordimer,

Tyler. There has seldom been a fiction writer of any worth who has not apprenticed himself to a master or masters while he learned his trade. Some have been fortunate enough to have their instructors alive and present—as fortunate as Maupassant when Flaubert used to criticize the young man's early stories before he threw them into the fire. But the splendid thing about apprenticeship in writing is that the masters—from all eras and many languages—are always on hand. They speak to the student from the page. The question is not whether anyone can teach you how to write fiction, it is whether you can learn.

There is something of a small paradox hidden in this. Great writers and good writers handle their craft extremely well on the whole, but no one is flawless. And, when a first-rate writer makes a wrong move, tries an experiment that doesn't work, or simply makes a technical blunder, the mistake stands out. Homer nods; Tolstoy tries to reach too far; Joyce comes a cropper. It is here that the young writer gets an unintended lesson quite as valuable as the correct kind.

The best and happiest way to learn would be to sit—as so many generations of young writers have done—at a café table in Paris listening to Stendhal, or Turgenev, or Joyce, or Hemingway debating technique with their friends. Every fiction writer who is at all good cares deeply about this matter. Every great writer knows something about it that no one else knows. But, since that café table isn't just down the street for most people, the nearest useful thing would be to have a book that brings together many writers' ideas about their craft, along with examples of how they solved, didn't quite solve, or failed to solve some of the technical problems of telling a story. We have tried to do that here.

This is not a how-to-do-it book. It is a how-it-was-done book—and also a how-it-wasn't-done book. The comments and examples are meant to suggest the eternal problems in putting a story together and making it work as a story.

There is a vast amount to be learned about technique from reading masterpieces of the novel or short story; unfortunately, there is far less to be learned from criticism. Literary critics often discuss a novel in terms of myth, symbol, irony, ambiguity, and other high matters while seeming ignorant of such fundamental ones as how the plot works, how characters are juxtaposed, or how the novel is constructed. The two classic books on technique are Percy Lubbock's *The Craft of Fiction* and E. M. Forster's *Aspects of the Novel*. But, in recent years, other fiction writers such as Eudora Welty, Flannery O'Connor, Jorge Luis Borges, and John Gardner have written on technique with new and interesting insights. The practitioners themselves remain the best analysts.

We have tried to make this a book of working information, suggestion, and example. Fiction, an art of many resources, has no absolute rules or laws. Its whole code of technique is built on precedent alone. Learning about it is a matter of finding out which methods seem to have succeeded or failed in the past. To describe this very flexible working practice, we have always tried to use the phrase "principles of fiction" rather than anything more restrictive. A principle is nothing more than a reasonable way of meeting one or another technical demand, and a principle's only sanction is that a considerable number of gifted writers seem to have followed it—to their advantage. Thus, the writer who does not is taking a gamble.

Fiction, of course, lives by taking gambles, risks, or long

shots as much as it does by traditional good sense. But, before he gambles, an author must know the difference between a justified risk and a pointless experiment. He must have a knowledge of principles before he can push beyond them.

For the special purposes of this book, we decided to abolish mortality and to regard all writers as alive and contemporaneous; therefore, do not be surprised to find Leo Tolstoy sharing a sentence with Ann Beattie or Alberto Moravia taking notes as Aristotle talks. There is no doubt that most of the craft of modern fiction comes out of that inventive era from the beginning of the nineteenth century through the early years of our own. But, on the other hand, the 1970s and 1980s have seen the appearance of a new generation of gifted writers. It is both instructive and agreeable to think of the best writers of all the years living together under the roof of Henry James's "house of fiction."

A note on words of gender in this book: We have followed the traditional custom of referring to "the author" or "the reader" as "he" rather than use the awkward "he or she" or "his or her" throughout. That usage is not meant to be sexist. We hope we have atoned by making plain our admiration for the many brilliant women who have practiced the art of fiction —perhaps in greater numbers today than ever before.

A note on this edition: This book was first published in 1964 and it remained in print for the next twenty years. During those two decades, a number of talented and innovative fiction writers have appeared. The novel—often written off as dead by critics in the 1960s—flourished anew, and the short story again became much written and much read in the 1980s.

This complete revision of *Technique in Fiction* was done in order to take as much as possible of the new fiction into account. About the inventiveness of its writers there is no question, and they deserve to be cited in a book like this one; however, those twenty years of fiction have not produced any bombshells of change in technique. There was no *Ulysses* or *Brothers Karamazov* to astonish us into believing that all the old principles were in question. If anything, the writers have demonstrated that old bottles and new wine can go very well together.

TECHNIQUE IN FICTION

SECOND EDITION: REVISED AND UPDATED FOR A NEW
GENERATION

ONE

CONCEPTION: THE ORIGINS OF A STORY

LOOKING AROUND AND LISTENING

The scene is a dining room in an English seaside hotel on a dreary Easter weekend when there are few guests:

> At last, and it was fitting that he should be the one to break the silence, the clergyman made an audible remark. Addressing the white-haired lady, whose table adjoined his, he said tentatively, "This must be a change from Uganda, Miss Fell."
>
> It was less than he deserved that she should be a little deaf, so that he was forced to repeat his not very brilliant observation, whose inanity she emphasized yet further by saying in a loud bright voice, "A change from Uganda—it certainly is!"
>
> "What a lovely title for a novel that would be," Dulcie whispered, and one can see that it would be almost easy to write. The plot is beginning to take shape already. . . .[1]

Dulcie, the central character in Barbara Pym's *No Fond Return of Love,* is not a writer, and the possibilities of a book called *A Change from Uganda* will never be explored. But here is an example of the wayward, unexpected manner in which ideas for stories come to the writer—while she (in this case) is spooning up soup, bending over a dropped napkin, or curiously surveying fellow guests. There is, of course, no aspect of fiction that worries the would-be writer more than that of conception. "Where can I get ideas?" is a frequent complaint, often followed by "Nothing interesting ever happens to me." What that person lacks is Dulcie's (presumed) quick ability to recognize the seed of a fiction and then to link imagined African experiences with this deaf old woman in the depressing English resort. It is essential that the writer train himself to look around and to listen.

One of the most famous anecdotes about literary conception is told by Henry James about an English woman novelist who wrote a striking story about French Protestant young people. The author was "congratulated on her opportunities for getting to know this particular way of life." Her opportunities, James says, "consisted of her having once, in Paris, ascended a staircase, passed an open door where, in the household of a *pasteur,* some of the young Protestants were seated at table round a finished meal." He adds that "the glimpse made a picture; it lasted only a moment, but that moment was experience."

The would-be writer might have a sour reaction to that anecdote, thinking that a momentary impression hardly gave the writer the authority to try to create a world she knew nothing of. James, however, explains a little further about the making of the tale. He says that the writer had got "her direct personal impression, and she turned out her type. She knew what youth was, and what Protestantism was; she also had the advantage of having seen what it was to be French, so that she converted these ideas into a concrete image and produced a reality."

It seems, therefore, that fiction originates in direct personal impression linked by imagination with the writer's resources of experience. This is a matter of looking and listening not just with eyes and ears but with intelligence and memory.

Both the moment in the seaside hotel and the episode on the staircase are examples of the writer seizing a subject out of someone else's life. The counterpart method is, of course, exploiting autobiography in fictional form. Many writers—Thomas Mann, Ernest Hemingway, Christopher Isherwood, and Mary McCarthy among them—have done it very well. But even the most varied and eventful lives furnish far less material than the world of others, and, sooner or later, the true fiction writer turns to theft.

Henry James, that majestic butler at the great table of Society, quietly pocketed ideas from country house, drawing room, or banquet gossip. Each was what he liked to call a *donnée*—something "given" to him. But, if he lifted these small treasures, he never took more than he needed. When the anecdote teller insisted on filling in all the details, James would recoil in horror and protest that he didn't want to know "too much."

"Too much" meant all the boring facts surrounding the little gleam of *donnée* that James's trained eye had picked out (the amateur writer would have listened to the whole of the tale and saved every scrap for the printed page).

In Joseph Conrad's *Nostromo,* anecdote, personal experience, and reading knowledge came together to make a magical mixture. Early in Conrad's seafaring career, he had heard about a man who had single-handedly stolen a whole shipload of treasure during a South American revolution. The bare anecdote did not interest Conrad at the time. Then, nearly thirty years later, he came across a volume of memoirs by an American seaman. A brief portion of it dealt with the author's experiences aboard a schooner whose master and owner was that same treasure thief of the old anecdote. The seaman described this man as "an unmitigated rascal, a small cheat, stupidly ferocious. . . ."

The chance confirmation of the old tale evoked in Conrad "the memories of that distant time when everything was so fresh, so surprising, so venturesome, so interesting; bits of strange coasts under the stars, shadows of hills in the sunshine, men's passions in the dusk, gossip half forgotten. . . ." Even with his anecdote fleshed out a little, Conrad still felt no urge to write: "To invent a circumstantial account of the robbery did not appeal to me." Then Conrad began to toy with the character of the thief. Perhaps he need not be a "confirmed rogue"? In fact, he might be a man of character, an actor and possibly a victim in the changing scenes of a revolution. At that moment, he had "the first vision of a twilight country which was to become the province of Sulaco, with its high shadowy Sierra and its misty Campo for mute witnesses of events flowing from the passions of men shortsighted in good and evil."

Thus, an impression for fiction can come from anywhere. There are no very special staircases, privileged anecdotes, or old volumes fate reserves for a few lucky writers. Astonishments are everywhere. The only luck lies in having—or in cultivating—what Elizabeth Bowen calls "susceptibility," which is simply the trait of looking hard at the life around one and relating it quickly to ideas, memories, or knowledge. Being susceptible means being a collector without a system. Anything that has the gleam of a story in it—conversations, a glimpse of a countryside, the sight of a face in the street—is to be taken home carefully whether it is of any apparent value or not.

Like any collector of old railroad lanterns, antique washbasins, brass military insignia, or ink bottles, the writer will soon get some gifts of other people's castoffs: "I have a wonderful idea for you . . ." or "With your talent, you could turn this into a fascinating book. . . ." But miracles do happen once in a while. Agatha Christie's most famous novel, *The Murder of Roger Ackroyd*, seems to have come from two unsolicited pieces of advice. Her brother-in-law, James Watt, complained that "almost anybody turns out to be a criminal nowadays in detective stories—even the detective. What I would like to see is a Watson who turned out to be the criminal." Agatha Christie mulled this over. "Then, as it happened, much the same idea was also suggested to me by Lord Louis Mountbatten, as he then was, who wrote to suggest that a story should be narrated in the first person by someone who later turned out to be the murderer." Not very many of us can rely on members of the royal family to send us ideas, however, and so it is that alertness, or self-training for Bowen's "susceptibility," which has to make do as a substitute.

One important way to increase that "susceptibility" is by use of what is called "lateral thinking." The concept was first expressed by the French writer Paul Souriau *("Pour inventer il faut penser à côté")* and is defined by Arthur Koestler as "a shift of attention to some feature of the situation, or an aspect of the problem, which was previously ignored, or only present on the fringes of awareness." Mathematicians have explained it as a way of discovering some America or other if you are trying hard to get to India. And Sir Alexander Fleming, discoverer of penicillin, noted the case of the inventor who set out to synchronize the rate of fire from a machine gun with an airplane propeller's revolutions—and discovered "an excellent way of imitating the mooing of a cow."

For the writer who learns to think sideways thus, there will be some cow moos, but there will also be a few new Americas. This kind of thinking depends on mental processes that are subjective, nonlogical, associational, uninhibited, and with a random quality. The result is not conceived until it is arrived at. William Butler Yeats tells a story about a time when he was living in London and was very homesick for Ireland. One day he was walking down Fleet Street and "heard a little tinkle of water and saw a fountain in a shop-window which balanced a little ball upon its jet and began to remember lake water. From the sudden remembrance came my poem 'Innisfree,' my first lyric with anything in its rhythm of my own music."

Here an aural impression and a couple of visual impressions quickly translated themselves into images of a cabin, the lapping water of a lake and a bee-loud glade. But the chief translation in the mind of the man standing on "the pavements grey" is from the oppressive city to the place "where peace comes dropping slow." There is something hypnotic about watching a ball balancing on the tip of a water-jet and —it would seem—Yeats let himself fall into that abstracted state in which associational thought, lateral thought, is so fertile.

THE USES OF NOTEBOOKS

Memory is often unresponsive. Despite desperate efforts, it won't bring back that fact or emotion or sensuous apprehension when needed. For this reason, many writers keep notebooks or journals and put down ideas or impressions while they are still fresh. Some have even collected "string too short for saving." Katherine Mansfield liked to record phrases or sentences that might come in useful to round off a paragraph in some yet-unwritten story. Chekhov, in his notebooks, has such jottings as, "Caressing her lover: 'My vulture,'" and Scott Fitzgerald kept fragments such as, "Long white gloves dripping from her forearms." Somerset Maugham used to complain that he would never live long enough to use up all the story or novel ideas in his notebooks. Henry James not only recorded the ideas but added possible ways of working them out into stories. Here are two examples:

Last evening . . . Miss R. said, after the conversation had run a little upon the way Americans drag their children about Europe: "A girl should be shown Europe— or taken to travel—by her husband—she has no business to see the world before. He takes her, he initiates her."

Struck with this as the old-fashioned French view and possible idea for a little tale. The girl whose husband is to show her everything—so that she waits at home—and who never gets a husband. . . .

This is a story that James apparently never wrote and, as such, is an example of the many entries that will serve no direct purpose. Here, however, in a much-abridged form, is the entry that led to *The Spoils of Poynton:*

> Last night at a dinner at Lady Lindsay's . . . Mrs. Anstruther-Thompson [told me this history]. It is a small and ugly matter . . . a little social and psychological picture. It appears that the circumstance is about to come out in a process-at-law. Some young laird, in Scotland, inherited, by the death of his father, a large place filled with valuable things. . . . His mother was still living, and had always lived, in this rich old house, in which she took pride and delight. . . . The son married . . . and went down with his wife to take possession—possession exclusive, of course—according to English custom. On doing so he found that pictures and other treasures were absent—and had been removed by his mother.[2]

James goes on to tell how the son protested his mother's high-handedness and how she responded by demanding still other possessions. There was a public quarrel that ended in the mother's announcing that her son was illegitimate—and hence not really the heir. James adds, "It presents a very fine case of the situation in which, in England, there has always seemed to me to be a story—the situation of the mother deposed . . . turned out of the big house on the son's marriage. . . ."

The evolution of *The Spoils of Poynton* from an anecdote told at a dinner party is too long to paraphrase here, but the reader will find it in *The Notebooks of Henry James,* a book that belongs in every writer's library. The development of the novel illustrates the immense change between the first conception and the execution. James kept the central fact of the feud only because he was aware of the danger of being confined by the details of an actual happening. Life, he said, is all "inclusion and confusion," and the point of any event is lost in the uproar. Art, on the other hand, is "discrimination and selection," and this point is its *raison d'être.* James found the scandal that disgraced the laird and his mother ugly and lacking finish. At the climax of *The Spoils of Poynton,* he sent the great house up in flames—a more meaningful comment on selfishness and the overvaluation of earthly goods.

Another advantage of the notebook is that the act of putting down ideas in coherent form is a kind of cooling-off process. Coming back to them later, the writer may wonder why they seemed worth preserving in the first place. The notebook is therefore a good place for winnowing.

Elizabeth Bowen remarks that "a man's whole life may be rendered down, by analysis, to variations upon a single theme." Thus, as the notebook gets thicker, a ruling passion, the main subject for the writer, will probably emerge. Learning to write often seems to include a lot of wasted motions. One of the most wasteful for a young writer is to commit a solander—and even to get it published. A solander is one of those hollow books made by cutting out the center of the pages and gluing the edges together. A good many established writers have turned out solander-fictions in their time.

When critics say that a writer is beginning to come into his own, they mean that he has finally learned and mastered the theme that swims, always in his unconscious. Taken all together, his most crucial notebook entries are fused, as it were, into the story he is uniquely qualified to tell. Sarah Orne Jewett said, "The thing that teases the mind over and over for years, and at last gets itself put down rightly on paper —whether little or great, it belongs to Literature."

For some writers, notebooks are no help at all. Ivy Compton-Burnett was scornful of Katherine Mansfield's store of fragments and said, "She said that she never knew when such things would come in useful, and I suspect she never found out." Compton-Burnett went on to say that she could not find notebooks of any use. She thought observing and eavesdropping on strangers pointless: "They are too indefinite and too much alike and are seldom living in anything but the surface of their lives. Think how rarely we should ourselves say or do anything that would throw light on our character or experience."

At the opposite extreme, some writers get overly dependent on the notebook. There is an exemplary story that comes from a letter Harold Laski, the British political scientist, wrote to Justice Oliver Wendell Holmes in 1930:

I went . . . to a dinner to meet Virginia Woolf, the novelist. She tickled me greatly; it was like watching someone organise her immortality. Every phrase and gesture was studied. Now and again, when she said something a little out of the ordinary, she wrote it down herself in a notebook.[3]

There is a delightful essay titled "Keeping a Notebook" by Joan Didion (in her book *Slouching Towards Bethlehem*). She says, "keepers of notebooks are a different breed . . . , lonely and resistant rearrangers of things, anxious malcontents, children afflicted apparently at birth with some presentiment of loss." She observes that her notebook has never been an accurate, factual record of what she has been doing or thinking, nor is it an objective record of what she has seen. It is more a way of preserving the self as it existed at any given moment in time. "Remember what it is to be me: that is always the point." Once the writer has got in touch with that self, it all comes back. "We are well advised to keep on nodding terms with people we used to be, whether we find them attractive company or not. . . . We forget all too soon the things we thought we could never forget. We forget the loves and betrayals alike, forget what we whispered and what we screamed, forget who we were."

So, she says, she abandoned the factual for what some would call lies. "The cracked crab I recall having for lunch the day my father came home from Detroit in 1945 must certainly be embroidery. . . . I was ten years old and would not now remember the cracked crab. The day's events did not turn on cracked crab. And yet it is precisely that fictitious crab that makes me see the afternoon all over again, a home movie run all too often, the father bearing gifts, the child weeping, an exercise in family love and guilt."

This, of course, is a very rigorous definition of a note-book's purpose, and it will seem too exclusive to many writers. But it does have the virtue of fixing on that most important function: the power to recover the former self in all its complexity and, through it, to relive the emotional past.

A BLINKING OF THE EYES

Turgenev once said that his stories originated in a vision of a person or persons who hovered in front of him and solicited his attention. Henry James, who has left us this account, added that Turgenev's task was to find for these characters "their right relations . . . to imagine . . . the situations most useful and most favourable to the sense of the creatures themselves, the complications they would be most likely to produce and feel." This process yielded Turgenev his story. James, who worked along similar lines, could not understand an author who saw his story first and then cast around for characters to populate it.

Although it is no longer very fashionable to admit it, many writers would agree with Turgenev in viewing the creative process as a kind of séance that summons presences from the timeless dark of the unconscious. Ellen Glasgow would certainly have agreed. Once, when she was asked why one of her male characters kept blinking his eyes, she answered, "I did not make him blink his eyes. He was blinking them when I first saw him, as a child, by the roadside."

Many other writers will speak privately of characters taking command of the story at some point. When the story is advancing well, there is a sensation of one or more presences hovering somewhere nearby and dictating the events of the fiction.

To put it another way, those are the times when intuition and imagination have been allowed to take over. The process is not quite so mysterious and occult as writers have often made it sound.

Ideas that come to the writer through family often carry a kind of blood tie that makes them seem more vivid and relevant. Even in this day of the nuclear family, there are still lore and legend and family portraits that might make or contribute to a fiction. One of the writers of this book has an aunt who, as a very young woman, lived next door to the redoubtable Susan B. Anthony (leader of the women's rights movement in the late nineteenth century). When the aunt later married a young Canadian farmer, the couple made their wedding journey to Rochester, New York, where Miss Anthony gave them a gala wedding supper. An author planning a story might ask what character he would give these two naive young people, what could be said of their uncomfortable and roundabout journey from rural Ontario to Rochester, what description might there be of their excitement and discomfort as guests of the famous and formidable woman? Did this notable event have any long-lasting effect on their lives? Or did it have none at all?

A VIEW OF SALISBURY

Anthony Trollope's autobiography was published in 1883, the year following his death; it very quickly damaged his reputation and reduced the sales of his novels—for a peculiar reason. The late Victorians still preserved a great faith in the power of inspiration, and, in his personal account, Trollope sounded less like an artist and more like a clerk-copyist. His gentle readers felt that he had taken all the grandeur out of the art of fiction and had reduced it to a timetable and so many pages' quota per day. He says, "It was my practice to be at my table every morning at 5.30 a.m.; and it was also my practice to allow myself no mercy. . . . By beginning at that hour I could complete my literary work before I dressed for breakfast. . . . It had at this time become my custom . . . to write with my watch before me, and to require of myself 250 words every quarter of an hour."

All of this was deceptive. Trollope's account of his clerkly working habits has really nothing to do with his imaginative accomplishments as a novelist, and his account of the genesis of the Barsetshire novels is particularly to the point here. Contrary to Henry James's opinion, Trollope shows how the subject of a story may be the original inspiration, with the concepts of the characters to follow.

As a General Post Office official, Trollope traveled often. One summer evening, he was wandering near the cathedral in Salisbury when he got the idea for *The Warden* (from which all of his ecclesiastical novels of Barchester descended). At the time, his idea had "no reference to clergy in general." He had been reading a newspaper controversy about the sources of clergy income.

As to his qualifications for undertaking such a subject, Trollope said, "No one could have had less reason . . . to presume himself able to write about clergymen. I have been often asked in which period of my early life I lived so long in a cathedral city as to have become intimate with the ways of a Close. I never lived in any cathedral city—except London —never knew anything of any Close, and at that time enjoyed no particular intimacy with any clergyman." He added that his characters came from his "moral consciousness" and what he picked up as he went along.

A subject, like characters, can emerge from anywhere. Rose Macaulay, a fine and underrated modern English novelist, said that one of her books "had its genesis in the reflection 'how manifold is human nature.' " She then thought it might be interesting to make one character seem to be two "as far thro' the book as was possible." Another novel came from her "brooding on Cambridge life as it was about 1640," and one of her last novels derived from "a meditation on Ruin, physical and material."

The danger in being abstract before one is concrete, in choosing a big subject before the story and characters are born, is a danger of disproportion. Thus, a novel in pursuit of an idea can turn into a propaganda essay. Other novels are devoid of human beings because they have somewhat the same intention as *The World Almanac*—fiction by Arthur Hailey and James A. Michener, for example. J. P. Marquand, the talented author of *The Late George Apley* and *Wickford Point*, later on turned from character to subject and produced some now-forgotten novels about banking, the military, show business, and so on. This is not meant to deprecate research, however. Its results can add all sorts of interesting verisimilitude and realism to the story—and in this information age, a vast amount of fact is available to the writer. But it must serve, not rule. There is a difference between a novel about some human beings who have chosen to be in the banking business and one about the banking business that must, by the rules of fiction, have some characters to carry it on. "I once knew this old banker in our town, and what a character he was! After forty years, he knew every trick in the book." Contrast that with, "Now, there are some very interesting trade secrets in banking and a neophyte has to learn them by experience."

The beginning writer is always told to write about what he knows, and he, in turn, may wonder what it is that he is supposed to know. How much did a merchant marine officer (Conrad) know about anarchists and revolutions? How much did a post office bureaucrat (Trollope) know about the life of the clergy? How much did a New Yorker (James) know about the feelings of a dispossessed Scottish dowager? Enough; they knew enough. Like Henry James's writer on the staircase, they connected some experience with some observation with some reading, and wove all that together by imagination.

The novice writer may sum up his or her life and find out that what he or she literally knows is how to grow up, to fall in or out of love, to learn something in school, to lose a father or mother, to go camping, to have a baby, to catch the flu. The writer suspects that is not enough; and it isn't.

The great fiction writers deal with the things that are common to us all—love, birth, death, folly—without being commonplace. But it is a mistake to believe that they deal with them out of their own immediate experience. What they are able to do is translate that private experience into a larger social context: to show what is universal in particular happenings.

No good fiction writer chooses his subject in cold blood. It is always something that appeals to him as a means of showing certain truths about the human condition. But then he must descend to the human condition and, in the words of W. H. Auden, "become the whole of boredom, subject to / Vulgar complaints like love, among the Just / Be just, among the Filthy filthy too, / And in his own weak person if he can, / Must suffer dully all the wrongs of man."[4]

TESTING IDEAS

Seed ideas for fiction are perverse things. One seems to transform into pure energy and the story almost writes itself. Then there are a hundred others with much the same promising look and feel. Taking one of these, a writer may stubbornly work on its development for days or months until he at last must realize that it is sterile. (Or—as sometimes happens—he may doggedly finish it and publish it.)

It is very advantageous but often difficult to divine early the difference between the good seed and the bad one. What was the difference between this entry in Albert Camus' *Cahiers* and many others?: "Today, mother died. Or it might have been yesterday, I don't know." In contrast with other notations, this one seized the writer's imagination and became the opening of Camus' novel *The Stranger.* We must suppose that this small example of the absurd suddenly gave the author a clue to the mind of Meursault, his alienated protagonist, and the novel flowed from that.

Perhaps the first question to be put to an idea would be: does it have some intimacy with my (the writer's) long-held beliefs or feelings or, as Joan Didion put it, does it touch some sensitive spot in the memory that makes it all come back? Is it closely associated with something that makes me angry, or sad, or delighted; is it something that would turn up in my dreams? Does it seem to have sought me out rather than the other way round?

Does it persist in the mind? Does it come back unbidden while I am making a cup of coffee or walking out to mail a letter? Does it wake me up in the middle of the night? Does it seem to grow, accumulating new details, new angles to view it? If I refuse to set down one word of it for three days, will it still be there tormenting me to write? And, finally, do I go to bed afraid I might die and thus the story or book would never get written?

This kind of reaction is the strongest possible signal, yet there may be other perfectly good story ideas that are not as immediately galvanizing—and there are other questions to test them. For example: does the idea have a second act? Few good stories are made out of a single situation alone, no matter how strong that situation might be. Does the idea lead forward to some development? Does it begin to suggest not just an event but a series of events to come? Does the simple concept seem to become more richly complex the more I think about it? Does the idea immediately begin to produce characters, real or imaginary?

Passing these tests is, of course, no absolute guarantee that the initial concept will end up as a first-rate novel or story, but, in dealing with the mystery of first causes, it is the best indication we have.

(There are also some false tests. Your aunt, when asked,

says that she thinks it is an old idea because she believes she has read something like it before. Your best friend fails to laugh at the funny parts. A friend who is also a writer says that it seems interesting enough but it will never sell.)

Notes to Chapter 1

1. New York: E. P. Dutton, 1961; p. 220.
2. New York: Alfred A. Knopf, 1960; p. 166.
3. *The Holmes-Laski Letters* (Cambridge, Mass.: Harvard University Press, 1953.) II, p. 1299.
4. *The Collected Poetry of W.H. Auden* (New York: Random House, 1945) p. 39.

TWO

BEGINNINGS

A short story is like a flare sent into the sky. Suddenly and startlingly, it illuminates one portion of the world and the lives of a few people who are caught in its glare. The light is brief, intense, and contrasts are likely to be dramatic. Then it fades quickly and is gone. But, if it is worth its moment of brilliance, it will leave an enduring afterimage in the mind's eye of the beholder. In contrast, the novel has great luxuries of time and space. It can explore without hurry, develop inevitable currents of action, and watch its people change and mature.

In the evolution of the short story, it thus became an accepted idea that the writer must choose a salient moment in the life of the story at which to part the darkness and begin. The activity, already in progress, must be revealed at just the instant that will best compel the reader's attention.

John Gardner begins his notable story "Redemption" this way:

One day in April, a clear, blue day when crocuses were in bloom, Jack Hawthorne ran over and killed his brother, David. Even at the last moment, he could have prevented his brother's death by slamming on the tractor brakes, easily in reach for all the shortness of his legs, but he was unable to think or, rather, thought unclearly, and so watched it happen, as he would again and again watch it happen in his mind, with nearly undiminished intensity and clarity, all of his life.[1]

It is, of course, the one violent and horrifying moment that is to generate a time of sorrow and guilt for father and son. It is meant to clasp us in tragedy at the very outset. But Gardner has overlooked an important principle about human empathy.

One is shocked at the news of a horrible accident reported in the paper or on television. A disaster in Mexico or Lebanon arouses feelings of pity. But, though we may be moved by them, these things carry no personal grief for us, no sense of our own actual involvement. And thus it is with Gardner's beginning. Two people we have never heard of before have been involved in a fatality. It is a news report. Gardner will thereafter have to struggle hard to overcome that alienation; he will have to make Jack Hawthorne our fictional intimate if we are ever to feel his guilt and sorrow. If we had known Jack and his brother David previously, in some happier and more ordinary time, we would have felt the death as the death of a friend—and Jack's guilt-ridden mourning could be understood almost without words. (And Gardner could have devoted more care to creating the "redemption," which, as it stands, is the least convincing part of the story.)

So it is that an attempt to capture the reader with one powerful stroke at the outset could be a handicap more than a benefit. Akin to this kind of beginning is something that is often called a "hook" in the magazine articles that offer "how to write for money" advice to beginning authors. Presumably, the fishlike reader is snagged by it and held captive to the end. Mystery, violence, strangeness of character or situation, some highly tantalizing suggestion of plot—these are the reliable lures to catch the innocent creature.

Queer and inexplicable as the business was, on the surface it appeared fairly simple—at the same time, at least; but with the passing of years, and owing to there not having been a single witness of what happened except Sara Clayburn herself, the stories about it have become so exaggerated, and often so ridiculously inaccurate, that it seems necessary that someone connected with the affair . . . should record the few facts known.[2]

This an example of a quite genteel hook as cast by Edith Wharton at the beginning of a story called "All Souls." It is not characteristic of Wharton's best work, and it turns out to be a promise unfulfilled because what follows is a commonplace ghost story with little suspense or invention. This kind of finger-crooking and breathless now-the-awful-truth-can-be-told attitude is usually a sign of worse to come.

A writer has to discriminate wisely between the attention-getting device that soon becomes fairly irrelevant to the story and the beginning that genuinely gathers the reader into the arms of the story.

Here is another story beginning:

As Gregor Samsa awoke one morning from easy dreams, he found himself in his bed, transformed into a giant insect. He was lying on his back, which now seemed so hard that it might have been armor-plated, and when he lifted his head a little, he could see his arched brown belly. It was divided into lateral plates so slippery that the bed quilt was about to slide off completely. His numerous legs, which were pitiably thin compared with the rest of his bulk, waved helplessly before his eyes.[3]

This is the famous first paragraph of Franz Kafka's "The Metamorphosis," and it has had a curious history. As the introduction to a tale that ranks with the best of Gogol or Poe, it was much singled out and admired by its first generation of readers. But a strange thing happened with the second generation—this horrifying, eerie paragraph—looked at in a different light, began to seem funny. Literary college students quoted it to describe their morning-after feelings. In parody forms, it appeared in magazine competitions. Comedians who had a highbrow audience used it for jokes. The shock of the Absurd had turned into the merely absurd. This did not, of course, prove that "The Metamorphosis" is a bad story, but it is an example of the risks of extreme or overcharged beginnings.

All this is by way of making a modest point—the story has its being in the mind of the author, and the beginning derives from it. An exciting, dramatic beginning is entirely possible, but it must be justified completely by the story that follows. Otherwise, it is likely to be irrelevant, specious, or, like poor Gregor Samsa, a bit ridiculous.

The most sensible way to approach the matter is for the

writer to establish some general controls before he puts down the first word. First, he should avoid the temptation to pack too much into the beginning of his story. All launchings are perilous—and it is best to do one thing at a time at first. A story that commences by trying to establish, almost simultaneously, three or four characters, hinting at their relationships, making them exchange ideas, setting up their milieu, putting them into dramatic action, and involving them in a plot is in trouble at once.

Here, for example, is the beginning of a first novel by a twenty-nine-year-old writer:

One Saturday in late August when my friend Olwen Taylor's mother telephoned to say that Olwen would not be able to go to the bioscope because she was going to a wedding, I refused to go with Gloria Dufalette (I heard Mrs. Dufalette's call, out the back door at the next house—Gloriah! Gloriah!) or with Paddy Connolly. —Paddy Connolly's little brother picked his nose, and no member of his family stopped him doing it.—4

In these few lines there are crammed seven characters (and two new ones appear in the subsequent paragraph). There are six activities, from the mother's telephoning to the boy's picking his nose. Yet none of this is of any significance for the novel to come, with one exception—the word "I." The only possible rationale for this start is that it may, perhaps, suggest a busy, small-town neighborhood. Other than that, it is a waste.

The beginning comes from *The Lying Days* by Nadine Gordimer, and its awkwardness simply shows that even one of the finest fiction writers of our time once had her difficulties in making an initial impression.

Another beginning:

Eyes closed, heart beating fast, fingers digging into the arm-rest, a prayer ringing in her head, by sheer force of will Laura had been able to get the plane up in the air and keep it there. Now it seemed to be doing reasonably well on its own and so she relaxed and opened her eyes. Her first plane trip had two hours and seven minutes to go before they would reach La Guardia airport, near New York City, and Laura, far away from her mother, her sister Bess, and her police lieutenant dad back at 178 Elm Street, Indianapolis, would be facing the big city alone. Not quite alone because there was the promise, in which Laura took little stock, that one of the Gibsons, probably Charley, a law student, whom she had never seen, would be on hand to meet her. But even though Martha Gibson was her mother's cousin, Laura had heard about the casual ways of rich people who lived in the 60's on Manhattan's Upper East Side and she was beginning to have misgivings about staying with them while she studied at the Manhattan Conservatory on her new, and highly prized, scholarship.

This is the beginning of a student story, and, obviously, the writer is trying to stuff the reader with information as quickly as possible. Addresses, occupations, financial standing, family relationships, attitudes, etc., are all too much to learn at once before any interest in Laura or the Gibson family has been established.

In most stories, time, place, a few characters, and a hint of drama are necessary elements to introduce early on, but the writer should know that not all of them have equal weight and value. Thus, the second control the author might observe would be a selection of those elements—whether of character, action, or involvement—that represents the deepest characteristics of his story and to begin with one of them. And here he should use all of his powers of definition. Laura is a very nervous and frightened young woman. She comes from an Indianapolis family made up of a police lieutenant father, a mother, and a sister named Bess. Which of these two sentences represents a thing that should define her when we meet her first, huddled in her airplane seat? Which can be postponed to some later point in the story?

Whether the writer begins slowly or rapidly, whether the story is to be realistic or fantastic, he cannot simply point at things or simply name them. However preliminary the definition may be—and however partial or misleading it may turn out to be later—he must use a clarity of line that separates his story and its entities from all the confused mass of the rest of the world.

Beginnings lead off, but they must also have the seeds of finality in them. And so there is another valuable control that the author might set up for himself: the habit of thinking a story through to its conclusion when deciding on the tactics of the beginning. While a half-conceived story may offer a great variety of possibilities for leading off, a story seen from the perspective of its ending will narrow those possibilities to the few most effective. Those few will be the ones most closely and richly involved with the matter and meaning of the story —and often these are the same ones that carry the most inevitability within them.

Here there must be an explanatory note. What we are

discussing is the whole process of the creation of a story through several drafts. A writer, of course, may begin with just a glimmer—a first thought that leads to others without any precise idea of where he will end (as noted in chap. 1). After another draft or two, however, he should have found the shape of his story and its appropriate ending. At that point, he can see his story "from the perspective of his ending" and decide whether or not his beginning is in harmony with his conclusion.

Many discussions of fictional technique raise false problems, and the problem of an "interesting beginning" as a thing in itself is surely artificial. If the writer has a story worth telling; if he has the finish well in mind as he begins his final draft; and if his introductory page (or pages) is thoroughly a part of the life of that story, he can be sure of himself. And he can be sure of his reader.

All of these controls are in the interests of economy, and, whether the writer intends to make some broad statement or to make some specific effect, he must not waste any of his story's brief life. What the beginning says must be relevant to the whole, but the manner is another matter. It can be chosen from the whole range of narrative methods in fiction: scenic description, character description, dialogue, summary of past events, action in the present, generalization, a letter, an interior monologue—or anything else. Although it is not recommended that a writer begin with a laundry list, an explanation of nuclear fission, or the preamble to the United States Constitution, any of these things could be used—if they functioned in the story and if they were handled with brilliance.

Nor is the writer limited to one method alone. In the course of its history, the short story has tended to acquire far more density and complexity than the simple tale from which it originated. Thus, it may be useful to introduce things by a mixed method at the outset. "The River," a story by Flannery O'Connor, begins this way:

> The child stood glum and limp in the middle of the dark living room while his father pulled him into a plaid coat. His right arm was hung in the sleeve, but the father buttoned the coat anyway and pushed him forward toward a pale spotted hand that stuck through the half-open door.
>
> "He ain't fixed right," a loud voice said from the hall.
>
> "Well then for Christ's sake fix him," the father muttered. "It's six o'clock in the morning." He was in his bathrobe and barefooted. When he got to the door and tried to shut it, he found her looming in it, a speckled skeleton in a long pea-green coat and felt helmet.
>
> "And his and my carfare," she said. "It'll be twict we have to ride the car."
>
> He went into the bedroom to get the money and when he came back, she and the boy were both standing in the middle of the room. She was taking stock. "I wouldn't smell those dead cigarette butts long if I was ever to come sit with you," she said, shaking him down in his coat.[5]

O'Connor has here used the mixed method of dialogue and description to produce a first impression of three characters and four different attitudes. There is the glum, limp little boy; the loud, critical baby-sitter; and the weary, indifferent father. By quick touches, we get a sense of the father's attitude toward the child, the child's attitude toward the whole situation, that of the father toward the woman, and that of the woman toward the household. Additionally—though we won't realize this until later—there is a sentence with much symbolical meaning for the story: "Well then for Christ's sake fix him."

Quite a lot is being developed at the same time, yet there is an order in this variety; all of the elements have a clear relationship to one another and to the whole. The writer is at ease with what she knows and is about to tell, and so she conveys to the reader a sense of being in the midst of fictional life.

THE NOVEL

A good novel is not merely a sizable short story. There is a qualitative difference as well as one of scale. Most writers come to the novel form after a certain amount of experience in writing short fiction and fail at first to recognize that they are now in a new country. This is as true of beginnings as of everything else, and the writer must get used to a number of subtle differences in two techniques that are also greatly akin.

Whatever the method, most modern short stories begin with brevity, compression, immediate significance. A novelist's thoughts are longer because he is not compelled to strike for the vital moments alone and because he is traveling either a greater or a slower journey within the span of birth to death. He is concerned less with effect than with engrossment. He must persuade his reader to enter the labyrinth.

More than that, he should begin with something that will capture a tone or a style of feeling that will echo throughout the book. A certain novel begins with some people in boats fishing dead men out of the Thames by lantern light. That opening is a portent; it casts its shadow over the whole long, loose course of the story. Another opens with a very succinct conversation between an English gentleman and his wife. They are discussing the themes of social status, money, and marriage: they have marriageable daughters. The novel will go on to explore these concerns in many ramifications. The beginning of a novel should have the power to persist and recur in the reader's consciousness.

Yet so many novels begin just anywhere, anyhow. The author is doing finger exercises at some mental keyboard; he is doing verbal calisthenics; or he is standing at the window smoking his pipe and giving us the benefit of his views on life. In chapter 2, he becomes desperate and buckles down to commence his story.

The beginning of a novel should be not only relevant in details but carefully chosen as to time. Where, in the long stretch of imaginary life, is the true point to begin? With the birth of the hero? That would seem to be the oldest and simplest answer. But an even older solution was to begin with the hero's ancestry and to work gradually toward his birth. Needless to say, these choices now seem archaic.

All novels have a past; all novels should live in a present of their own. Somewhere in the flow of time, the writer must draw the visible line between the past—a resource for memory—and what is (in the "novelistic present") taking place before us. In doing so, he must remember that only that part of "then" that has a bearing on "now" is worth being told. In itself, the fictional past is dead. It lives only insofar as it shades, energizes, or explains something in the present.

There is a very old and trustworthy narrative principle called "in medias res"—to begin one's story "in the middle of things." This is simply to say that a novel ought to begin within the context of the events it intends to deal with. It ought to give an intimation of those events at the very start. (The word "event" is used very broadly, meaning not just happenings but any kind of motion-development in the story.)

Bernard Malamud's fine novel *The Fixer* begins just that way:

> From the small crossed window of his room above the stable in the brickyard, Yakov Bok saw people in their long overcoats running somewhere early that morning, everybody in the same direction. Vey iz mir, he thought uneasily, something has happened. The Russians, coming from streets around the cemetery, were hurrying singly, or in groups, in the spring snow in the direction of the ravine, some running in the middle of the slushy cobblestone streets. Yakov hastily hid the small tin can in which he saved silver rubles, then rushed down to the yard to find out what the excitement was about. He asked Proshko, the foreman, loitering near the smoky brick kilns, but Proshko spat and said nothing. Outside the yard, a black-shawled, bony-faced peasant woman, thickly dressed, told him that the dead body of a child had been found nearby. . . . The next day, the Kievlyanin reported that in a damp cave in a ravine not more than a verst and a half from the brickworks, the body of a murdered Russian boy, Zhenia Golov, twelve years old, had been found. . . .[6]

That murder, of course, is to become the most important fact in Yakov's life and the source of the whole novel. The choice of beginning is so exact and natural that it might seem to be the only one. Yet a novelist less capable than Malamud might have made his beginning fit the answers to other questions: Should I first tell my twentieth-century readers what a shtetl was and what it looked like? Or—if my story is to be largely about virulent anti-Semitism, should I begin with an incident to illustrate Russian intolerance toward the Jews? Or—if Yakov, the fixer, is to be my hero, should I first make the reader acquainted with him and his personal history? Instead, Malamud defined for himself exactly what the "in medias" of the story is and what the "res."

Many nineteenth-century novelists—including quite a few good ones—could not bear to represent themselves in the opening pages of their books as writers of fiction. Rather, they pretended to be landscape painters, essayists, antiquarians, historians, or whatever. One famous example is Balzac posing as an inventory taker. At the beginning of *Père Goriot,* Mme. Vauquer's boarding house is detailed foot by foot, with all its furnishings, its floor plan, its guest list, and even its smells:

The ground-floor, necessarily part of the house where the affairs of such an establishment are carried on, consists, first, of a parlor lighted by two windows looking upon the street, which is entered through a glass door. This, the common sitting room, leads to the dining room, which is separated from the kitchen by the well of the staircase, the steps of which are of wood, square and polished. Nothing can be more dismal than this sitting room, furnished with chairs and arm-chairs covered with a species of striped horsehair. In the center stands a round table with a marble top. . . .

This dining room is pervaded by a smell for which there is no name in any language. . . . It suggests used air, rancid grease, and mildew. It strikes a chill as of malaria to the bones; it penetrates the clothes with fetid moisture; it fills the nostrils with the mingled odors of a scullery and a hospital. . . .

The whole room is a depository of worthless furniture, rejected elsewhere and gathered here, as the battered relics of humanity are gathered in hospitals for the incurable. Here may be seen a barometer with a hooded monk who steps out when it rains. . . .[7]

There are eight pages like this of nothing but things. It is only on page 11 that we finally come to "Eugène de Rastignac—such was his name—was one of that large class of young men . . ." It is a slow, cumbersome, laborious, overdetailed inventory of a beginning. Of course, it is all wrong; any writer would be mad to introduce his story this way.

But in Balzac's case, there is another factor to be considered: he was a genius. One of the odd things about genius is that it can sometimes combine all its disasters to make a brilliant success. Somehow Balzac managed to touch all of those inanimate objects with life and to breathe an air of expectancy into that empty house. A little later, the reader realizes that this is the hell of drabness and despair that Eugène must flee in order to live; all the rest of the book is an escape attempt.

Balzac—just barely, and against heavy odds—comes off with the gamble. His success is, nevertheless, one of those infrequent exceptions to a good principle—the principle that a piece of fiction ought to begin to move forward at its very inception. In the range of fictional possibilities, there is room for the set piece: extended descriptions of a scene or a character, interior monologues, lore of one kind or another. Yet these are static; the novel has to pause for them and standing still is generally a poor way to set out.

Compare Balzac's conception of his nineteenth-century reader with a conception of the modern reader held by Robertson Davies. This is the beginning of Davies's estimable novel *The Manticore:*

"When did you decide you should come to Zurich, Mr. Staunton?"

"When I heard myself shouting in the theatre."

"You decided at that moment?"

"I think so. Of course I put myself through the usual examination afterward to be quite sure. But I could say that the decision was made as soon as I heard my own voice shouting."

"The usual examination? Could you tell me a little more about that, please?"

"Certainly. I mean the sort of examination one always makes to determine the nature of anyone's conduct, his degree of responsibility and all that. It was perfectly clear. I was no longer in command of my actions. Something had to be done, and I must do it before others had to do it on my behalf."[8]

About his reader, Balzac assumed this: he had never been in a run-down Parisian boarding-house (or, probably, any boarding house), and he had little imagination about one.

Davies, on the other hand, assumes that his reader will detect small clues and thus be able to fill in what the writer has left unsaid. With scarcely any effort, the reader deduces:

1. That the person with whom Mr. Staunton is talking is a psychiatrist (Mr. Staunton has an emotional problem and Zurich is a center for Jungian psychiatry).

2. That Mr. Staunton is probably Anglo-Saxon (by his name).
3. That he is well educated and well-to-do (the first by the way he speaks and the second by the fact that he can afford to come some distance to consult a psychiatrist).
4. That he is, ordinarily, a responsible and well-balanced person (because he is so alarmed at an outbreak he considers irrational and has sought treatment).
5. That he is an analytical man, perhaps a member of some profession (he speaks of "the sort of examination one always makes").
6. That he is a decisive man (because the moment after his strange action in the theater, he decided that he must see a psychiatrist).

Because he left all of this rather mundane but necessary information implied, Davies has been able to draw a quick sketch of his central character and, at the same time, to move briskly into his story.

Wuthering Heights begins: "I have just returned from a visit to my landlord—the solitary neighbour that I shall be troubled with." Emily Brontë gives us a good look at the bleak, windswept house and several glimpses of Mr. Heathcliff, the handsome but rather surly owner. She does not try to give much of a direct characterization of him, but she hits on a superb idea for indirect characterization. When Heathcliff leaves for a few minutes, the room is suddenly filled with menacing dogs. The narrator is attacked by "a ruffianly bitch" and "half-a-dozen four-footed fiends of various ages and sizes." And it becomes clear that the temperament of the master—fierce, savage, suspicious—is demonstrated wordlessly by his dogs. The beginning suggests Heathcliff's violent emotions and the violence to come in the story, although he does nothing more than invite the narrator in, offer him a glass of wine, and converse with him for a while.

It is the image that succeeds so well, not any particular sentence or phrasing. But there are openings that sound out like a bell simply because the words are so memorable and so evocative:

Call me Ishmael. [Herman Melville, *Moby-Dick*]

Garp's mother, Jenny Fields, was arrested in Boston in 1942 for wounding a man in a movie theatre. [John Irving, *The World According to Garp*]

In mid-journey along the path of our life, I found myself in a dark wood and the true way was lost. [Dante Alighieri, *The Divine Comedy*]

It was the best of times, it was the worst of times, it was the age of wisdom, it was the age of foolishness, it was the epoch of belief, it was the epoch of incredulity, it was the season of Light, it was the season of Darkness. . . . [Charles Dickens, *A Tale of Two Cities*]

He was an old man who fished alone in a skiff in the Gulf Stream and he had gone eighty-four days now without taking a fish. [Ernest Hemingway, *The Old Man and the Sea*]

Stately, plump Buck Mulligan came from the stairhead, bearing a bowl of lather on which a mirror and a razor lay crossed. [James Joyce, *Ulysses*]

In each one of these, there is a current of energy that comes through the words, and, without much exaggeration, it could be said that they do the same thing that the initial lines of good poems do—give the first pleasure and the first shock of anticipation.

Perhaps one of the most famous of all beginnings is that of Tolstoy's *Anna Karenina* because it is such an elegant example of oblique prophecy; it has very little to do with the book's plot and everything to do with the book's thematic meaning:

> Happy families are all alike; every unhappy family is unhappy in its own way.
> Everything was in confusion in the house of the Oblonskys. The wife had discovered that the husband was carrying on an intrigue with a French girl, who had been a governess in the family, and she had announced to her husband that she could not go on living in the same house with him. This position of affairs had now lasted three days, and not only the husband and wife themselves, but all the members of their household, were painfully conscious of it. . . . The wife did not leave her own room, the husband had not been home for three days. The children ran wild all over the house; the English governess quarrelled with the housekeeper. . . .[9]

On its surface, this seems to be a précis of a little domestic drama, given in swift strokes and meant to outline the recent turn of events with the Oblonskys. The opening has nothing to do with any of the main characters to appear later—Kitty, Levin, Anna, Karenin, or Vronsky. But Tolstoy is transmitting a subliminal meaning at the same time. It is a long foreshadow of the future, or a hidden clue to the thematic essence of the book. This is going to be a contrasting story of happy and unhappy families. "All was in confusion in the house"—it is to be a story of domestic and emotional confusions. And it will be a story in which the fact of adultery plays a major part.

Though the "subliminal" opening is a kind of omen, the patent opening is useful to lead off the story of the Oblonskys' "little problem." The reader discovers Stepan Arkadyevitch stirring comfortably on a sofa in his study, waking, up, and remembering a delicious dream—a fine dinner served on glass tables that sang an aria, some sort of little decanters, women present. He smiles happily, gets up, reaches for his dressing gown—and only when he finds it not there does he remember that he is in his study, and why. The personal life of the novel begins.

Probably the simplest mechanism for giving the beginning and ending a common significance is something called an "envelope." The envelope is the outer wrapping of story within which lies another story. In the best novels that use this device, not only do the beginning and ending form the two sides of an envelope but the inner and outer stories are interdependent as well. A most interesting example of this is Flaubert's novel *Madame Bovary*.

As everybody knows, it is the story of a woman's great romantic illusion and disillusion—thus, why does it begin with the account of a dull, awkward, clownish boy's first day in school? Charles Bovary is to be the butt of every joke in class. It is a vivid little scene and it makes its point well, but the purpose seems obscure because, as the reader soon learns, the story is to have no primary business with Charles or his schooldays. It is to be the adult story of his wife and her love affairs. Charles is oblivious of nearly every one of these situations that are the heart of the novel. He exists in the novel, but he does not live in it; and he does not change at all.

In the back of the reader's mind, therefore, is lodged the unanswered question of why Emma is not brought forward at first for some quick and unforgettable impression. It would be easy enough to establish the simple fact of Charles's stupidity later on when they first meet. Thus, the beginning seems to be a piece of carelessness.

It is not. Flaubert was the most calculating of novelists, and he weighed every scene many times. When the reader arrives near the end of the novel, he discovers that it does not close with Emma's death by poison but with an account of the desolate last months of Charles's life. And here is an illumination. The reader finally understands the significance of the beginning: the start and finish reinforce each other. Charles is unwilling and unable to recognize how completely destructive his wife had been—this was the "deed of fate," he tells one of her former lovers.

Thus, a story that begins with a dazed and clumsy schoolboy ends with the dazed and clumsy man, still unable to comprehend what life has done to him. The pattern of Charles's character has been the whole background of the small world against which Emma has tried vainly to rebel. Symbolically, his ineptness and stupidity are the great, enveloping facts of the story, which Flaubert has emphasized by giving Charles the two symbolic positions. It is one of the clearest examples of a view across the distance from beginning to end. Not only does Flaubert see it that way, but he forces the reader to see it that way as well.

INSERTING INFORMATION AT THE BEGINNING

The inexperienced writer often finds it hard to deal with what-has-gone-before as he starts his story. Imagine that the whole history of the matter he's writing about stretches from A to G. Where to start—with the twinkle in Zeus's eye, the rape of Leda, the birth of Helen, the judgment of Paris, the rape of Helen, the wrath of Achilles, Achilles and Hector before the gates, or the Wooden Horse?

Say that he wisely chooses, in medias res, the wrath of Achilles. At that point, the drama has begun to mount. He must now, like the author of the student story quoted above, find a way to transmit the knowledge of those events that have gone before. In playwriting, there is an ancient device for doing this, and it is full of ancient pitfalls. Two minor characters—servants, neighbors, family acquaintances or such—appear first on the stage and hold forth with a loaded conversation. Here is one bad example:

BARTENDER: Yep, it sure will be good to have Doc Pfeiffer back from the Veet-nam war. Gonna be a big day.

FIRST DRINKER: Him? Why, he must be close to seventy —and besides, I seen him here in town just last week. Looked bad, too.

SECOND DRINKER: No, he means young Doc, the son. Gone must be about two years now. Old Doc took over the practice again, at his age, and now I hear he's about wore out what with the work plus all that trouble.

THIRD DRINKER: I just wonder who's gonna tell Ed junior about his wife, Susie.

BARTENDER: Probably some big mouth who keeps bringing the subject up.

THIRD DRINKER: Hey, it's not like I'm the only one. Bill Shaw's daughter who works over at the Lakeview Motel seen her and Joe Perkins, her boss at the Apex Paint Company, coming out of one of the—

BARTENDER: We've all heard those stories. Some people ought to have their mind washed out with soap.

SECOND DRINKER: Seems like some guys just get bad luck stored up for them. First, Susie Pfeiffer goes off the tracks and then old Doc gets hit with that malpractice suit.

THIRD DRINKER: I always said he was too old to do them complicated operations. But the worst thing was nobody smelled his breath before they let him go into the operating room.

This (admittedly exaggerated) dialogue has people exchanging information in an artificial way. They are briefing the audience rather than talking naturally among themselves. Too much plot, too compressed, and too soon.

A more successful way employs a kind of sleight of hand. The writer directs the reader's attention to something in process and, gradually and unobtrusively, slips the facts of his fictional case into the narrative. It is often a good idea to take advantage of the reader's capacity for inference and do this obliquely. Half of the information in Robertson Davies's *The*

Manticore beginning is implied. Brontë directs one's attention
to the ferocity of Heathcliff's dogs—knowing that most people think that dogs reflect the personalities of their owners.
Stepan Arkadyevitch awakes from a wish-fulfillment dream,
relishes it, and only then remembers the unhappy situation
he has caused. The reader infers at once that the cause of the
confusion in the house of the Oblonskys is Stepan's thoughtless self-indulgence.

An old journalistic axiom rules that all news stories
should very quickly answer the questions *who, when, what,
where,* and *how.* The novelist usually tries to answer them
without seeming to. The interesting events in progress take
the foreground and the *who-when-what-where-how* orientations
arrive almost subliminally.

The question of *who* is answered very simply and ade-
quately for the moment at the beginning of *Anna Karenina*—
an upper-class Russian family with an irresponsible father.
The novelist must avoid crowds and be careful with casts.
Crowds are faceless and unanimated names coming all at
once. Members of the cast are people who must begin to
breathe for the reader without elaborate descriptions. Nothing moves while a portrait (interior or exterior) is being
painted. In the beginning, the human facts are best limited
to two considerations: some knowledge of the characters (or
a character) according to their situation in life (Texas bank-
ers? A Maine fisherman's family?) is the first. Some knowledge of the character or characters by individual traits—but
only the simplest and most motivational ones—is second.

One kind of beginning favored by novelists in the past
was the cameo scene in which two or more characters were

introduced simultaneously and shown in a conversation or some initial kind of action. Thus, Edith Wharton's *The Custom of the Country* starts off with a scene in which a pretty and quite spoiled young woman treats her indulgent mother and a visitor with marked rudeness.

With the right kind of control, this can be a useful way to lead off. It may have fallen out of fashion with novelists because it is such an obvious borrowing from the theater and, ineptly done, it can seem stagy. Most novelists of this era prefer to begin with a low-key description or the introduction of a single character, then lead on into the presence of other characters.

A good example of a dramatic scene that is meant to delineate only one character is the beginning of Muriel Spark's 1970 novel *The Driver's Seat*. A young woman is trying on a dress in a clothing shop. It is "patterned with green and purple squares on a white background, with blue spots within the green squares, cyclamen spots within the purple." For obvious reasons, no one has bought it, but this customer likes it very much. She is just about to buy it when the salesgirl tells her that the fabric is a new stainless kind. In a fury, the customer strips the dress off, shrieking, "Do you think I spill things on my clothes? Do I look as if I don't eat properly?"

The customer is a woman named Lise who is about to set out on a very strange journey—and the incident in the shop gives us several clues about a disturbed and reckless personality. The question of *who* is thus answered sharply and vividly.

The writer's problem of answering *where* and *when* may

have various degrees of difficulty. Scenes and times that are familiar to most readers can be identified easily:

> The village of Duc Pho in the distance straddled Highway 1 like a fuzzy patch sewn into the green quilt of the landscape. To the east of Duc Pho was a low mountain that separated it from the dull gleam of the China Sea's expanse. The last time he had been here, the mountain was surrounded by rice paddies; now, as the C-130 came in for a landing, he could see the air base at the western foot of the mountain and the perimeter of a camp as big as a city that stretched out eastward toward the sea.

But if the setting happens to be Chandrapore, India, in the 1920s or Jamaica in the 1860s, place names and topical references have little use. In such a case, the novelist often feels that even more surroundings and topography are required. E. M. Forster begins *A Passage to India* conventionally, with a view:

> Except for the Marabar Caves—and they are twenty miles off —the City of Chandrapore presents nothing extraordinary. Edged rather than washed by the River Ganges, it trails for a couple of miles along the bank, scarcely distinguishable from the rubbish it deposits so freely.[10]

Forster then proceeds to draw a verbal map of his small fictional territory. Place, because it is so alien to most of his readers, must come before events. In another kind of novel, the procedure might be simply wasteful or dull, but here it is essential. The description of locale, the feeling for place are things that ought to grow throughout the novel (as they do in Forster's small masterpiece).

The author who wishes to set his story in the past ought to establish his period fairly soon and rather casually. The standard ways of doing this are by reference to distinctive dress, customs, means of transportation, events of the time, contemporary names known to history, and so on. But nothing should be forced. A conversation about the Stamp Act or a description of a speakeasy should not be introduced just to pin down a date; they should be there only if they have importance to the stories in which they appear.

Now and then, a writer boldly solves all this in his title. There are: *The Last Days of Pompeii, 1984,* and *Count Belisarius*, all of which are precise clues to time. On the other hand, there is the misleadingly titled *During the Reign of the Queen of Persia*, which takes place in northern Ohio farm country in the 1950s—and, thus, the reader cannot trust a playful author. "It was one of the hottest days of the summer of 1835" is the first sentence in Turgenev's *On the Eve*—a direct if not very subtle solution.

But the all-important thing about the first stage of any fiction is that the author makes certain promises there. A successful novel will bear out those promises. The author should be in full command of his conception, not drifting hopefully toward it. He may promise wit and precision in the analysis of human relations (as Margaret Drabble does at the start of *The Ice Age*), a striking view of desolation (as does Tim O'Brien with his list of the dead and how they were killed at the beginning of *Going After Cacciato*), a surreal vision of life (as Franz Kafka does at the beginning of *The Trial*), or whatever other tenor the novel will have. In a certain sense, every beginning is (or should be) a symbol. On the strength of what the symbol promises, the reader commits himself to the story.

This has a bearing on the questions of *what* and *how*. There should be some sense of forward movement at the outset of a story or novel, but that does not mean that the beginning has to lead into the first act of a drama or even that it contain signposts pointing to the plot. The reader, starting out with no previous knowledge and no context from which to judge, will not recognize the relative importance of the things he is being told. Significance in fiction—as in life— is a cumulative matter. Recall the flawed beginning of John Gardner's "Redemption." Reflect on the news that your closest friend has suddenly won a million dollars in the state lottery—which will produce in you a complex series of emotions and associated ideas. The news that someone with a German name somewhere in Pennsylvania has had the same luck will produce a very low level of interest.

The author's strongest position is when he is leading toward some meaningful moment in his story. Such moments are best when they are a culmination of all the words, small acts, and silent clues that have gone before them. On the other hand, if the writer chooses to begin at some important dramatic point in his plot, he is then at the psychological disadvantage of having to proceed away from something rather than toward something. It is good to suggest to the reader that his greatest interest lies in the future. Henry James once wrote to Mrs. Humphry Ward, commenting critically on one of her novels:

I think your material suffers a little from the fact that the reader feels you approach your subject too immediately, show him its elements, the cards in your hand, too bang off from the first page—so that a wait to begin to guess what and whom the thing is going to be about doesn't impose itself: the antechamber or two and the crooked corridor before he is already in the Presence.[11]

But these remarks are not meant to forbid the author from beginning with something that later might have a part in the development of his story, nor do they deny him the choice of beginning with an action. They are simply cautionary suggestions against too much, too fast, and too soon.

"HIGH" AND "LOW" BEGINNINGS

There is a related, though quite separate, decision for the author to make. That is the matter of what "tone" to sound in the opening of the fiction. Imagine this as the tone of voice in which the author is speaking. If it is casual, unhurried, quiet, somewhat discursive or humorous, it might be called a "low" tone. For instance, here is the opening of Vladimir Nabokov's novel *The Real Life of Sebastian Knight*:

Sebastian Knight was born on the thirty-first of December, 1899, in the former capital of my country. An old Russian lady who has for some obscure reason begged me not to divulge her name, happened to show me in Paris the diary she had kept in the past. So uneventful had those years been (apparently) that the collecting of daily details (which is always a poor method of self-preservation) barely surpassed a short description of the day's weather; and it is curious to note in this respect that the personal diaries of sovereigns —no matter what troubles beset their realms—are mainly concerned with the same subject. Luck being what it is when left alone, here I was offered something which I might never have hunted down had it been a chosen quarry. Therefore, I am able to state that the morning of Sebastian's birth was a fine, windless one, with twelve degrees (Réaumur) below zero . . . this is all, however, that the good lady found worth setting down.[12]

Another example—with a somewhat different effect—occurs in *Ragtime* by E. L. Doctorow:

In 1902 Father built a house at the crest of the Broadview Avenue hill in New Rochelle, New York. It was a three-story brown shingle with dormers, bay windows and a screen porch. Striped awnings shaded the windows. The family took possession of this stout manse on a sunny day in June and it seemed for some years thereafter that all their days would be fair and warm. The best part of Father's income was derived from the manufacture of flags and bunting and other accoutrements of patriotism, including fireworks. Patriotism was a reliable sentiment in the early 1900's. Teddy Roosevelt was President. The population customarily gathered in great numbers either out of doors for parades, public concerts, fish fries, political picnics, social outings, or indoors in meeting halls, vaudeville theatres, operas, ballrooms. There seemed to be no entertainment that did not involve great swarms of people. Trains and steamers and trolleys moved them from one place to another. That was the style, that was the way people lived.[13]

Probably a majority of all novels begin in some similar quiet tone. It is a reliable way to make the reader feel easy and familiar in what is, after all, a highly artificial medium. In the first example, the main intention is not so much to inform the reader about Sebastian Knight as it is to win interest in a narrator who speaks with informality and charm. This would be a mistake if it amounted to nothing more. As the book progresses, it becomes clear that the personality of the narrator and his manner of thought are important to the shape of the story.

The second example—a private instance of the times sliding into more public observation—maintains the same level tone. Nothing startling, intense or even very important is happening. But, once Doctorow has set the scene of 1900's American comfort and complacency ("There were no Negroes. There were no immigrants"), he begins to introduce some more disquieting signs of the times. There is the sensational murder of Stanford White, the famous architect, by Harry K. Thaw. There is a glance at Emma Goldman, the revolutionary, who vehemently points out that there *are* Negroes and immigrants in America, and so on. Thus, without perceptibly raising his pitch, Doctorow manages to suggest rumors of trouble, which, for the moment, are far off from the warm, fair days on Broadview Avenue in New Rochelle.

For other purposes, a novelist may sometimes choose a "high" beginning. Here is one from Shirley Hazzard's *The Transit of Venus*:

By nightfall the headlines would be reporting devastation. It was simply that the sky, on a shadeless day, suddenly lowered itself like an awning. Purple silence petrified the limbs of trees and stood crops upright in the fields like hair on end. Whatever there was of fresh white paint sprang out from downs or dunes, or lacerated a roadside with a streak of fencing. This occurred shortly after midday on a summer Monday in the south of England.

As late as the following morning, small paragraphs would even appear in newspapers . . . unroofed houses and stripped orchards being given in numbers and acreage; with only lastly, briefly, the mention of a body where a bridge was swept away.

That noon a man was walking slowly into a landscape under a branch of lightning.[14]

The vision of this storm has many touches of melodrama—in fact, seems to promise melodrama to come. But, on the contrary, it simply serves to bring into the story Ted Tice, who is about to arrive at a country house well soaked but quite serene. There is, apparently, a more distant purpose for the ominous weather in the beginning because this is to be a story of unsettled loves and stormy emotions. The author has intended to suggest a symbolic atmosphere of electricity and danger with such words as "devastation," "petrified," and "lacerated." The real, external weather in the beginning would appear to stand for what will occur as "the weather of the heart" later on.

But there is another, much more obscure, bond between beginning and ending. In the closing scene, Ted Tice is saying good-bye to Caroline, his love, who is boarding a plane to Rome. She gets on, and notices a familiar figure—an ophthalmologist who had once treated her in New York. Then the plane takes off, and the description of that is loaded with almost as many portentous words as the beginning: "Within the cabin, nothing could be heard. Only, as the plane rose from the ground, a long hiss of air—like the intake of humanity's breath when a work of ages shrivels in an instant; or the great grasp of hull and ocean as a ship goes down." Those are the final words. Presumably, the plane is now heading for Rome, because we are told nothing to the contrary.

That is, nothing to the contrary unless we are the shrewdest of readers and have noted one sentence that occurs forty pages earlier: "Three months later he [the doctor] was to die in a plane crash on his way to an ophthalmologist's congress at Rome." It is a clue to the violent language of the final page—which is, we now see, deliberately parallel to the tone of the beginning.

The device does not work. Hazzard is a fine writer, the novel is a very good one, and the attempt to transmit a meaning through the tone of the language is an interesting experiment. The unfortunate thing is that the explanation rests on that one small gimmick, the author intruding as a fortune-teller of the future. It makes a great deal of difference to the reader's total impression of the novel as to whether the beautiful Caro is temporarily parted from her lover or whether she is about to die a terrible death.

The beginning of André Malraux's modern classic *Man's Fate* finds Ch'en, a terrorist, standing in a dark hotel room about to murder a sleeping man. It is a scene exotic enough for a Len Deighton or a Frederick Forsyth novel of suspense. Yet Malraux brings it within the realm of realism by concentrating not on the violence but on Ch'en's inner feelings— what goes through the mind of an intelligent man who must, against all his instincts, do murder for ideology's sake? Even at that, many readers might be alienated at the outset of this political novel by having too much of the bizarre thrust upon them. The "high" beginning, like any other, must find a way to engage the reader and make his interest endure beyond the momentary excitements.

CHOOSING THE BEGINNING

The writer who has laid out the main lines of his story either on paper or in his mind probably ought to worry a bit and question himself about finding an absolutely right beginning. For example, here might be some of the alternatives that would have to be winnowed. Say that his story is to focus largely on one woman's life and character. Should the reader meet her and get a strong impression in the first pages? Or should she be withheld for a short time—as Tolstoy withholds Anna Karenina and Flaubert Emma Bovary—while certain things in her milieu are examined?

Say that another story has to do with the relationships of four people over the course of a decade. Should it begin with their first meeting and proceed chronologically? Or might it be better to choose a moment, perhaps in the tenth year, when they are about to have some decisive change in their relationship—with only the relevant parts of the past recalled?

Say that one's story is about a lucky man who is also a fraud. He goes from one unearned success to another but finally has a catastrophic downfall. Should the beginning reflect the sunny and untroubled start of his career? Or should the author find indirect ways to suggest that this man carries within him the seeds of his destruction? All of these situations are oversimplified, and yet they do suggest some of the alternatives that have to be calculated before the writer makes that most important of moves, his first.

"Once upon a time in a faraway country there lived a handsome prince." Some of the best stories in the world began that way. But, sad to say, we are too old for them now. If the novelist or short story writer can arouse just half the anticipation the child had when he heard those words, he is in luck.

Notes to Chapter 2

1. From *The Art of Living and Other Stories* (New York: Alfred A. Knopf, 1974), p. 3.
2. From *Ghosts* (New York: Appleton-Century-Crofts, 1937), p. 3.
3. From *The Complete Stories* (New York: Schocken Books, 1971), p. 89.
4. New York: Simon & Schuster, 1953; p. 9.
5. From Flannery O'Connor, *The Complete Stories* (New York: Farrar, Straus & Giroux, 1971), p. 157.
6. New York: Farrar, Straus & Giroux, 1966; pp. 3, 4.
7. Katherine Prescott Wormeley, trans. (Boston: Little, Brown & Co., 1899), p. 6.
8. New York: Viking Press, 1972; p. 3.

9. Constance Garnett, trans. (New York: Random House, 1939), p. 3.

10. New York: Harcourt, Brace & World, 1924; p. 7.

11. *The Letters of Henry James* (New York: Charles Scribner's Sons, 1920), 1:322.

12. New York: New Directions, 1959; p. 12.

13. New York: Random House, 1975; p. 3.

14. New York: Viking Press, 1980; p. 3.

THREE

STYLE AND SPEECH

THE RIDDLE OF THE FEATHER

"Style," wrote George Sampson of Cambridge University, "is the feather in the arrow, not the feather in the cap."

That characteristic aphorism, by a man who was himself a notable stylist, suggests that style should not be a panache to decorate the work but a control that makes the shaft of meaning fly true to the center of the target. It suggests, as well, that the work of the stylist is like the work of the fletcher —a careful gluing of the trimmed feathers into thin grooves to make a mere pointed stick into a graceful and efficient missile.

To stretch the metaphor just a little further—many archers have arrow feathers of individual colors. In *The Elements of Style* by E. B. White and William Strunk, White says: "Every writer, by the way he uses the language, reveals something of his spirit, his habits, his capacities, his bias. This is inevitable as well as enjoyable. . . . No writer long remains incognito." Katherine Anne Porter amplifies that statement when she calls style "the writer's own special way of telling a thing that makes it precisely his own and no one else's."

White and Porter express every writer's central concern —that is, to produce stories and novels no one else could have written in quite the same way, bearing a personal signature throughout. This is far less a matter of fresh turns of rhetoric as of the achievement of a "voice" with the author's personality in it.

But is that individual voice, once discovered, a thing that the writer can automatically employ? Not at all. Many writers, even the best of them, sometime overlook the plain fact that one cannot say anything personal or very original about the wrong subject. No matter how practiced the stylist, the colors die and the music goes flat if he is stubbornly attempting the wrong thing. Katherine Anne Porter was one of the finest short fiction (novella and story) writers of the century, and *Flowering Judas* and *Pale Horse, Pale Rider* are dominated by a marvelous voice. Later on, she labored for more than twenty years to finish a novel called *Ship of Fools,* and, through many rewritings of her recalcitrant subject, she finally produced a mere bestseller—in a commonplace style and with only a trace of her voice. The moral is clear enough: a writer working at what he uneasily senses to be a trite or derivative subject cannot summon a freshness in his writing.

Here are some examples of able writers at work on subjects that defied or bored them.

He took a step towards her. She was seized with panic. He looked sinister and menacing. His gaunt face was distorted with hatred and those dark, deep-set eyes flashed. She made an effort at self-control. She was still holding the bag in her hand: she snatched the revolver and pointed it at him.

"If you don't go at once, I shall fire!" she cried.

"Fire then."

He took another step towards her.

"If you come an inch nearer, I shall shoot."[1]

• • •

The cars behind him hooted persistently; they hooted and hooted. At what? he asked. Suddenly he realized that they were hooting at him. The light had changed; it was green now; he had been blocking the way. He started off with a violent jerk. He had not mastered the art of driving in London.

The noise of London still seemed to him deafening, and the speed at which people drove was terrifying; but it was exciting after Africa. The shops even, he thought as he shot past rows of plate-glass windows, were marvelous. Along the kerb, too, there were barrows of fruit and flowers. Everywhere there was profusion; plenty. . . . Again the red light shone out; he pulled up. . . .[2]

• • •

Rev. Which Therefore . . . looked as spruce as an onion, wearing an off-white shirt of satinet with Wildean flounces at the sleeves. He had eyes the color of clarified butter, showing a kind of flexibility and openness betrayed neither by his slight but energetic body nor his volleyballshaped head that looked like the full, round topside of an Harrovian boater. His hair was thinning somewhat, often prompting recollections, uninvidious to be sure, of St. Nichodemus of Thyatria, patron saint of bald heads, who was circumspectly martyred by having a goatskin nailed to his pate with a tenpenny nail. Which welcomed the chances to go clubbing with Mother, never bruised the gin, and believed in the importance of being earnest. He had, in short, the soul of an interior decorator. . . .[3]

• • •

Yogi Johnson walked out of the workman's entrance of the pump-factory and down the street. Spring was in the air. The snow was melting and the gutters were running with snow-water. Yogi Johnson walked down the middle of the street, keeping his eye on the yet-unmelted ice. He turned to the left and crossed the bridge over the Bear River. The ice had already melted in the river and he watched the swirling brown current. Below, beside the stream, buds on the willow brush were coming out green.

It's a real chinook wind, Yogi thought. The foreman did right to let the men go. It wouldn't be safe keeping them in on a day like this. Anything might happen. The owner of the factory knew a thing or two. When the chinook blew, the thing to do was to get the men out of the factory. Then, if any of them were injured, it was not on him. He didn't get caught under the Employer's Liability Act. They knew a thing or two, these big pump-manufacturers. They were smart all right.[4]

Three of these authors were capable of much better work (and, of course, Hemingway was joking). The first two passages show writers trying to deal with something they cared little about telling. They are grimly pushing their way through an assignment and thoughts of style have been abandoned.

The first quotation comes from *Up at the Villa*, a short novel by Somerset Maugham. It illustrates how boring a string of declarative sentences can become, especially when they are built of clichés. Maugham found himself in the midst of a situational cliché and, having no personal response to it, borrowed sentences from detective stories or movie dialogue to fill the void.

Maugham told his friend Glenway Wescott that *Up at the Villa* was "done for money," although in his semicritical *Summing Up*, he might almost have had a defense of the novel in mind when he declared that "the artist is absorbed by his technique only when his theme is of no pressing interest to him. When he is obsessed by his theme, he has not much time to think of the artfulness of his presentation." Glenway Wescott found a kind of morbid interest in the story because he thought that the principal male character was based on Maugham's longtime lover, Gerald Haxton, and that the theme of blackmail had something to do with Haxton's hold over Maugham. If that was so, the book gains a bit of extra-literary interest, but no other.

Maugham's statement that an obsessive theme compels the writer to ignore artfulness is highly questionable. A first draft may be set down at top speed and roughly written if the writer feels that he will lose the emotion or the important details by polishing individual sentences. But that first draft must never be considered more than a mock-up of the final work to come.

Virginia Woolf's failure is more admirable because her struggle at least produced a novel of substance with many fine passages. The difficulty seems to be one of getting into strange and unfriendly waters. In *The Years*, she had hoped to go beyond the small, closed world of her earlier fiction. In her diary, she wrote, "It's to take in everything, sex, education, life, etc.: and come, with the most powerful and agile leaps, like a chamois, across precipices from 1880 to here and now." When the novel finally appeared in 1937, bad reviews succeeded the good ones, and she ended by changing her metaphor from the soaring chamois to that of an "odious rice pudding . . . a dank failure."

The passage quoted is, of course, supposed to show the

impressions of a man who is suffering from a small culture shock in London traffic, but the author has failed to imagine that except in the most banal way—which is reflected in the style. It begins with the redundancy of the two sentences about the hooting cars, then follows shortly with the redundancy of "He started off with a violent jerk. He had not mastered the art of driving in London." Next comes a slightly blurred impression of the street with its shop windows and barrows of fruits and flowers, and that has the seed of a good perception. A bad driver in heavy traffic is not going to notice details of what he's passing. But the perception is spoiled by the commonplace rendering. The shops are "marvelous" and the fruits and flowers are a "profusion." The scene and the emotion are dulled by the words. There is no single sentence that produces a shock of recognition. Anyone could have written the passage.

The third quotation is from Alexander Theroux's novel *Three Wogs*. It is, to be sure, a comic novel in which part of the humor comes from excess, yet it is quite possible that the style was more laughed at than laughed with. It is a style reminiscent of J. P. Donleavy and some other exuberant writers of the 1960s and 1970s.

One of its troubles is immediately apparent—the avalanche of metaphors. Look at what this clergyman is composed of: an onion, a touch of Oscar Wilde's dress, butter, a volleyball, a straw hat, a martyr's legend. Then there are two references to Oscar Wilde, one to hagiography, and one to a well-known English public school. The bad results of such an extraordinary mixture of notions come out in sentences like this one: "He had eyes the color of clarified butter, showing a kind of flexibility and openness betrayed neither by his slight but energetic body nor his volleyballshaped head that looked like the full, round topside of an Harrovian boater." First we get those shiny, yellow, liquid eyes that, rather miraculously, show "a kind of flexibility and openness." But that flexibility and openness isn't apparent in his "slight but energetic body," whatever that may mean. And, further, the flexibility and openness is not visible in the head that—take your choice—is like either a boys' school straw hat or a volleyball. The outcome of this kind of thinking is the sentence that seems to be complex and elegant but, on close examination, turns out to be a string of nonsequiturs. This is often the fate of writers who try for the ornate and the whimsical at the same time.

The fourth quotation is, admittedly, a parody. It is from Ernest Hemingway's *The Torrents of Spring* and it was meant to lampoon Sherwood Anderson's style. Yet because Hemingway learned his choppy prose rhythm from Anderson, it can also stand as a parody of Hemingway—and a whole generation of clipped-style realists that followed. Those sentences are short. They tell the truth. Sometimes it is a very boring truth. Sometimes we wish we had not heard the truth. Then we are caught by surprise when there is a sudden lyrical touch that blooms before our eyes like the buds on the willow brush coming out green. Then back to telling the truth.

A word must be said about those writers whose work is a permanent part of our literature in spite of showing no facility with the language. Theodore Dreiser managed to produce major novels in a ponderous, clumsy, Teutonic English. Sinclair Lewis captured a significant part of American life in a style no more sensitive than Dreiser's. Melville's *Moby-Dick*, according to D. H. Lawrence, is badly written: "At first you are put off by the style. It reads like journalism. It seems spurious. You feel Melville is trying to put something over you. It won't do. . . . Nobody can be more clownish, more clumsy and more sententiously in bad taste than Herman Melville. . . ."

The beginning writer must remember that a good style is nourished by good reading. With a true writer, the critical process is constantly at work whether he realizes it or not. He cannot fail to ask himself why Author A speaks directly and urgently to him whereas Author B does not. Although they have much the same kind of subject, why does one seem so vivid and the other so flat? Contrast Virginia Woolf's description of the driver in London traffic with her donkey-riding travelers in *The Voyage Out*:

> The midday sun . . . was beginning to beat down hotly. The higher they got the more of the sky appeared, until the mountain was only a small tent of earth against an enormous blue background. The English fell silent; the natives who walked beside the donkeys broke into queer wavering songs and tossed jokes from one to the other. The road grew very steep, and each rider kept his eyes fixed in front of them. Rather more strain was being put upon their bodies than is quite legitimate in a party of pleasure. . . .[5]

Aside from a couple of grammatical improprieties, this is effective writing. There is a good sense of both the labor of a steep trail and a gradual emergence into empty heights of sky. All is well until we reach that final, weak generalization. Use of the passive in place of the active voice is always a feebler way of stating things. Combine that with a rather prissy worry about whether the English tourists were straining themselves by riding up the mountain in the sun (what about the donkeys under them; what about the "natives" on foot?) and you have one of those letdown sentences that spoils a good paragraph.

The Voyage Out was Virginia Woolf's first novel, and it displays some of the beginner's ineptitude along with some of the stylistic talent that was to be so evident in her later work. The novice should read closely to be aware of how his predecessors have used language. That will provide a set of mental examples of what sort of style seems to work and what doesn't. And it is best to choose, in the way of predecessors, those authors most sympathetic in outlook, temperament, interests—and ability to make a sentence do what the imagination wants it to do.

It is this kind of experience that T. S. Eliot is describing when he speaks of "the influences which, so to speak, first introduce one to oneself." These influences offer "a form of expression which gives a clue to the discovery of one's own form." Eliot adds that authors who affect us most powerfully in our early days are probably not among "the great masters," who are "too exalted and remote. They are like distant ancestors who have been almost deified." We are more likely to learn from the lesser writer "who has directed one's first steps, is more like an admired elder brother." Eliot, himself, dedicated "The Waste Land" to "Ezra Pound, Il miglior fabbro" ("the better craftsman"). In the next stage of his experience, the new writer will probably find a model in some greater artist.

This last stage of apprenticeship is the most difficult of

all. The great influences can be less like elder brothers than like father figures whose domination is both baleful and beneficial—and very hard to shake. Major writers (almost always) develop and perfect a decidedly individual voice and mode of expression. A generation ago, there were many indentured servants to Henry James. Writing classes used to be full of the sons of Thomas Wolfe. Virginia Woolf, Faulkner, and Hemingway have had their stylistic followers. In the recent era of American Jewish writing, many young writers have learned the tones and the moves of Saul Bellow and Isaac Bashevis Singer.

Because the bright beginner is alert to the possibilities of language, he responds enthusiastically to the pronounced stylist. It is easier to pick up the rhythms and mannerisms of William Faulkner than of a plain writer like Anthony Powell. When he sees something original and striking, the beginner says, "That's it; that's the way!" and immediately starts to apply that kind of language to his own subject. The process of enthusiasm, infatuation, and disillusion can be very hard on writers. There comes a point when results of the "influence" of the master suddenly seems no more than bad imitation and the young writer feels stripped of all guidance. But, if he persists, he is likely to emerge from this despair with a slowly growing ability to speak in his own way, with a voice of his own.

THE WAYS OF SPEAKING

Different writers who declare on the subject scarcely ever agree on what "style" is and what its uses are.

Style, said Flaubert, is "itself an absolute way of seeing things." At another time, he said, "A good prose sentence should be like a good line of poetry—unchangeable."

"When we encounter a natural style, we are always surprised and delighted, for we thought to see an author and found a man," Pascal said.

"I have never taken any very great pains about writing," H. G. Wells declared. He said that it was not "jewellery" but "it has quite other aims than perfection, and the more one thinks of 'how it is done', the less one gets done."

"The whole secret of a living style," wrote Thomas Hardy, "and the difference between it and a dead style, lies in not having too much style—being in fact a little careless, or rather seeming to be, here and there."

And, finally, a pronouncement from Samuel Johnson that has been quoted to Oxford undergraduates since the eighteenth century: "Read over your compositions, and where ever you meet with a passage which you think is particularly fine, strike it out."

Pronouncements like these could be multiplied, but they would do little more than amplify three common attitudes toward style: that it is everything; that it is only important enough to be dismissed; that it must give an effect of naturalness and spontaneity. Along with these is the general rule that style should be neither awkward enough nor mannered enough to draw attention to itself and distract from the narrative.

In practice, the majority of writers manage a combination of all three theories. The most that can be safely said is that some writers are more acutely aware of the resources of language than others are. One of those who was painfully, compulsively aware of them was Flaubert, and he is generally credited with the dictum of *le mot juste*—exactly the right word to be chosen. Beyond that was the exact rightness of phrase and sentence. That concern, he thought, would produce an ideal style "as rhythmical as verse and as precise as science, with the booming rise and fall of a cello and plumes of fire . . . a style which penetrates the idea . . . like a dagger-thrust." Flaubert had other ideas about style that may seem rather fussy today. He decreed that there should be no assonance in prose; he thought no word should ever be repeated in the same manuscript page. But he is essentially right about working hard to find *le mot juste*, even if it is scarcely guaranteed to create iambics like science that sound like a cello, send off flames, and stab the idea—certainly a show worth waiting for.

Here is the kind of bad example Flaubert had in mind. It is a passage from *The Mysteries of Udolpho*, one of those copious novels of the eighteenth century:

> The peasants of this gay climate were often seen on an evening, when the day's labour was done, dancing in groups on the margin of the river. Their sprightly melodies, *débonnaire* steps, the fanciful figure of their dances, with the tasteful and capricious manner in which the girls adjusted their simple dress, gave a character to the scene entirely French.[6]

The author, Ann Radcliffe, is taking some pains to establish the setting of her story. But can we see those peasants? Can we visualize a dance going on in front of us? What way of adjusting a dress is "tasteful and capricious"? What kind of dress is simple? The author, as we might expect, even gets her French word wrong—*débonnaire* means very sweet, compliant, or good-natured, and it is hard to think of the difference between a good-natured and a bad-natured dance step. Finally, what if she had said, ". . . gave a character to the scene entirely Hungarian?" We should never have known the difference.

Although English literature from the sixteenth century to the nineteenth produced much admirable and varied prose, fiction writers were generally content to express themselves in a conventional language. The idea that a story could—like a poem—be embodied in some extraordinary style was slow to take hold, and the notable experiments with language have come chiefly in our century. James Joyce, of course, towers above all other experimenters, and *Finnegans Wake* is one of the few novels that pushed language to its extreme and yet endures. There have been others such as Gertrude Stein, John Hawkes (at times), Donald Barthelme, and William S. Burroughs. On the whole, readers in the second half of the twentieth century have much preferred an accessible style and, at the same time, have been much more tolerant of bizarre or forbidden subjects than past generations.

One problem a writer sometimes sets for himself is that of suspending his own natural style in order to adapt his language to that of a narrator or protagonist. Thus, Mark Twain assumes the voice of Huck Finn to relate *Huckleberry Finn* or Alice Walker speaks in the voice and sensibility of Celie in *The Color Purple.* These very successful style impersonations could not have been exceedingly difficult for either author. But there could be problems that require much more virtuosity—for example, a sighted author who tries to write a story from the dark, colorless, nongraphic world of a blind person. Or another who wishes to adopt the persona of an old man or woman of quite a different race and culture. Or another who decides to speak from the viewpoint of a character with limited intelligence.

A successful example of fitting style to mentality is Daniel Keyes's short novel titled *Flowers for Algernon.* In it, a mentally handicapped young man is enabled to raise his IQ dramatically as the result of an experimental operation and therapy. The story is told first in the language of a retarded person, then, as the cure begins to work, the language gradually becomes more sophisticated and literate until, at last, he is speaking and thinking as a genius. Here he is at the beginning of the book:

> I werk in Donners bakery where Mr Donner gives me 11 dollars a week and bred or cake if I want. I am 32 yeres old and next month is my birthday. . . .

Later on, Charlie is able to express himself in this way:

> Deep in the heat of my anger was forged an overwhelming insight into the thing that had disturbed me when Strauss spoke and when Nemur amplified his data. They had made a mistake—of course! The statistical evaluation of the waiting period necessary to prove the permanence of the change had been based on earlier experiments in the field of mental development and learning.[7]

Flowers for Algernon—and, similarly, the opening of James Joyce's *A Portrait of the Artist as a Young Man*—is an exceptional case of creating a style to fit a condition. But, even in more usual circumstances, style should be responsive to subject. Ellen Glasgow said wisely, "Style should be [like] a transparent envelope which changes color in response to the animation within."

One thing that tends to make the envelope opaque is the straining after a literary use of words. Willa Cather commented on a group of romantic storytellers saying, "They always departed in that school of writing; they never went anywhere." This might be called the Roget's Thesaurus school: "Don't just go, depart; don't just avoid, eschew; don't say 'then' when you can say 'at that point in time.' " Along with that, we Americans still have a lingering notion that euphemisms are more proper than the rude words for which they stand. Although sexual words and blasphemy are seldom disguised nowadays, writers will frequently choose such words as "perspire," "powder room," "prevarication," "nude," "ethnic," "liquidated," "terminated," and "disadvantaged" to somehow soften unpleasant or sensitive meanings.

Still another kind of stylistic failure occurs when a writer tries to use too much current slang or current neologisms. Vogue language dates very quickly, and what is trendy today is embarrassingly dated—or unintelligible—tomorrow. ("Hot snakes!" she exclaimed. "That's the cat's pajamas! I'm all of a doodah.")

On the whole, the great movement in American fiction since the 1920s has been toward an informal, colloquial, conversational style. Writers like Sherwood Anderson, Hemingway, and John Cheever gave it impetus; the *New Yorker*'s fiction and comment had a wide influence; books on usage by E. B. White and William Strunk and by Jacques Barzun demanded plain speaking. The norm of literary language in America has moved closer to the norm of everyday spoken language than ever before.

In the 1980s, there appeared a new movement that has been called "minimalist." The novelist Madison Smartt Bell has defined it thus: "It may fairly be described as a school because its representative work contains, as if by prescription, a number of specific elements: a trim, 'minimal' style, an obsessive concern for surface detail, a tendency to ignore or eliminate distinctions among the people it renders, and a studiedly deterministic, at times nihilistic, vision of the world."[8]

Bell cites as members of this "school" Raymond Carver, Ann Beattie, Amy Hempel, David Leavitt, Frederick Barthelme, and Bobbie Ann Mason. As well as minimal, Bell uses "stripped-down," "emaciated," and "anorexic" to describe their writing style. He says that a good deal of this derives from Hemingway's passion for excluding as much as possible from a story. ("If a writer of prose knows enough about what he is writing about he may omit things that he knows and the reader, if the writer is writing truly enough, will have a feeling of those things as strongly as though the writer had stated them. The dignity of movement of an ice-berg is due to only one-eighth of it being above water." [From *Death in the Afternoon.*]) Bell notes that Hemingway imagined, and omitted, whole life histories for the characters in "A Clean, Well-Lighted Place," and that "those unspoken elements of the story add to its force, but in its myriad contemporary imitations the unspoken has simply been left unthought."

It may be difficult, of course, for a reader to contemplate what isn't there and decide that the void represents a "whole life history" or merely something that was "unthought." One cipher looks very much like another cipher. It would be more accurate to say that Hemingway is good at furnishing hints, implications, even innuendoes, about the characters' otherwise-withheld lives. Though the prose may be bare and stripped of detail, the clues are many. When one waiter in "A Clean, Well-Lighted Place" tells the other that the old man tried to commit suicide from despair, the other asks what the despair was about. "Nothing," says the first waiter. "He has plenty of money." That tells us nothing provable about the old man, but it tells a lot about the first waiter's dismal outlook on life.

It is the mark of modern style, then, to make a few allusive words do in place of fuller explanations. Bell is rather too sweeping in his condemnations—Raymond Carver at his best, for instance, is shrewd at making the reader infer past lives or unspoken attitudes. But there is also truth in what Bell says about the level, black-and-white style of the new minimalist fiction. For instance, most of these writers try to avoid metaphors. When Bobbie Ann Mason uses one—"The highway was like the ocean. It seemed to go on forever and was a similar color"—it is deliberately flat and unexpressive (although it is meaningful to the story).

Writers of the previous generation dwelt on "significant" detail. The visual notes or small actions were put in to contribute to a sense of mood, a touch of character, or a slight complement to the general idea of the story. Stephen Crane's fiction was a kind of touchstone-reference for this and his "The Open Boat" furnished splendid examples of precise detail, beginning with its opening sentence, "None of them knew the color of the sky." Perhaps the most telling sentence in the story follows shortly: "These waves were most wrongfully and barbarously abrupt and tall, and each froth top was a problem in small boat navigation." It not only echoes the crew's bitterness at what fate is doing to them but suggests the constant struggle they were having to keep the boat on course against the sharp, oncoming waves.

Contrast this with a description from Frederick Barthelme's novel *Tracer:*

> I always liked parking lots, especially big ones at dusk, or at night, the way they look, all that open space, the glass in the cars shining, reflecting the lights; different kinds of lots, landscaped ones with cars on different levels, slopes painted with bright directions, box trees plump and squat, and wide open ones that stretch hundreds of yards in every direction, punctuated with store signs in harsh colors and careful letters, or curious, circus-like letters that sizzle against dark buildings or ink-blue sky; and they're wonderful when it rains or when it has rained because of the way the light splinters and glitters all over the place . . . and because of how it sounds on a cool night when a car rolls through a puddle nearby, or when two or three shoppers walk past, talking, their voices distinct but not quite decipherable, or when there's a breeze going in fits across the blacktop, blowing paper cups in manic half circles, rolling a soft drink bottle. . . .[9]

Now, this is excellent evocative description, almost a cinema verité scene. It is also one of those paradoxical modernist celebrations of what has always been assumed to be utilitarian-ugly, the American parking lot. (The narrator has found nothing in Florida that aroused anything like this loving description.) The difference between this and Crane's seascape is that the parking lot is, appropriately, no more than a transitory stop in the narrator's memory. Nothing happens there. In a moment, he will head for the airport to get a plane out. None of the fine detail is significant; it is simply present.

To a certain extent, the minimal style has become the favored style of the 1980s, even in the work of writers (Anne Tyler, for example) who are not at all minimalist writers. It has its Spartan virtues, but it also has its Spartan vices as a writing method.

SPEECH

"All good dialogue . . . ," says Elizabeth Bowen, "deals with something unprecedented." Dialogue should never be an exchange of commonplaces designed to feed the reader information. It is seldom suitable for describing persons or places; it is no substitute for direct narrative; and individual speech is useless as a vehicle for the philosophical brooding of the hero or heroine.

Brevity in dialogue is generally a virtue:

"What about the song? Why does that make you cry?"
"I am thinking about a person long ago who used to sing that song."
"And who was that person long ago?" asked Gabriel, smiling.

"It was a person I used to know in Galway when I was living with my grandmother," she said. . . .

"Someone you were in love with?" he asked ironically.

"It was a young boy I used to know," she answered, "named Michael Furey. He used to sing that song. . . . He was very delicate."[10]

This is the closing scene of Joyce's great story "The Dead." A man and wife are alone together in their room; the snow is falling outside. She is telling him for the first time about an early lover. A beginning writer might be tempted to have the wife go on indiscreetly, at length, about memories of Michael Furey. Or, on the other hand, he might make her very tight-lipped, after the first slip, and show her husband trying at length to interrogate her. But Joyce knew the exact limits of what he wanted to do in this dialogue. He evokes Michael Furey through the quick questions prompted by the husband's jealousy and the wife's spare, reluctant answers. Here we have "something unprecedented" in the revelation of a past love, in the revelation that the wife still thinks nostalgically of him, and in the revelation of the husband's jealousy. Few stories can bring so much to light with so few words, but the writer's concern is always to produce at least one unprecedented something that adds to the reader's knowledge of situation or character or event.

Speech is necessarily selective. The routine social exchanges of "How are you?"; "Please sit down"; "Would you like coffee or tea?"; "Is your cold better?" should either be omitted or, if they have something to do with the situation, summarized briefly:

Having seen Mrs. Pence into her favorite chair and provided her with coffee laced with whiskey and honey to ease her susceptible throat, Mrs. Flood sat down opposite her old friend and, leaning forward expectantly, said, "You didn't telephone. I suppose that means the worst?"

To be selective also means to eliminate repetition from fictional conversations. In real life, many people are habitual repeaters: "As I always say . . ."; "Don't forget that you promised to . . ."; "I believe I've told you about the time I was. . . ." Most of us are incapable of reporting an event without telling parts of it over three or four times in an effort to cover every detail. And there are always those who tell you what they're going to tell you, then tell you, and finally tell you what they've told you. Unless they are cast as caricatures, such people are outlaws from fiction.

There are those writers who write dialogue too well. They have a quick ear for idiom and inflection, they can make printed speech sound quite natural, they can keep the level of interest up—but they have two vices: they don't know when to edit or when to stop. George V. Higgins very often brings his story into a working-class bar where a couple of Boston Irishmen are debating or plotting something. The exchanges are wonderfully lifelike and the reader becomes a next-barstool listener. But the talk, much of it, is simply for talk's sake, something to fill the empty spaces in life, something to kill the evening. To be sure, there will be a plot that emerges and there is an objective (often criminal), but the neighboring barstool may be deserted before that becomes clear.

It is not that dialogue is supposed to be coldly economical and efficient. It does have use for the calculated random remark (as seen in stories by Eudora Welty or Donald Barthelme) or entertaining digressions, but it should never stray too far or become prolix.

One of the most important purposes of speech is to express character. Barbara Pym captures the principal qualities of her two major figures, Dulcie and Aylwin, in this scene from *No Fond Return of Love.* Dulcie is introducing Aylwin to her dinner guests, who include her lodger Viola, a middle-aged woman unnervingly devoted to Aylwin, and Maurice, Dulcie's former fiancée:

"I think you know everybody except Maurice Clive. This is Dr. Aylwin Forbes," she explained to Maurice.

"I should think that you must be pretty busy at this time of the year," said Maurice, "with all this 'flu about."

"Oh, he's not that kind of a doctor," Dulcie explained. . . .

"Ah, I see. Then you must be one of the learned variety," said Maurice.

"Yes, perhaps you might call it that. Learned but useless," said Aylwin with a little laugh. "I don't heal the sick, I'm afraid," he added, almost as if he despised those who did.

"But you do such really worth-while work in your own way," said Viola fussily. "It's so vitally important that the standard of true scholarship should be kept up, when you think of all there is to be contended with nowadays."

"You mean television and the general lowering of standards everywhere?" said Maurice politely.

"Yes, that among other things," said Viola rather darkly. "Aylwin's book on Edmund Lydden will be the definitive study."

"Edmund Lydden," Maurice repeated. "Ah, yes."

"Who is he?" asked Laurel, feeling that she was the only person young or old enough—in her case young—to ask such a question.

"Edmund Lydden is—I suppose we should say was—one of the little band of neo-metaphysical poets of the late seventeenth and early eighteenth centuries who have been neglected by posterity," said Aylwin, beaming at Laurel and wondering if he ought to explain the term "neo-metaphysical." . . .

"I shouldn't have thought Edmund Lydden left enough poetry for it to be worth writing about him," said Dulcie. "Surely there can't be much?"

"That may be," said Aylwin, "but what remarkable stuff it is! The 'Winter' sonnets—unfinished, admittedly—and the three Epithalamia, not to mention the fragments."

"Ah, yes, the fragments," murmured Viola, throwing him an intimate glance.[11]

This is capsule characterization. It pins down certain traits in the space of a scene. Generally, the evidence accumulates from scene to scene (as Barbara Pym, both earlier and later in this novel, accumulates evidence of Aylwin's uncertain vanity and Dulcie's vacillation between delicacy and bluntness).

Neither the author nor the character shows his hand directly. Both of them have an interest in keeping up appearances. In another fiction, let's say that the question arises whether Robert is something of a con man. Robert certainly wouldn't have told you himself, and his creator was holding that back, letting you think of him as a nice guy, until it dawned on you—just before it began to dawn on Janet. Then all those rather odd remarks he'd been making and his stories that didn't quite ring true come together in your mind. What now strikes Janet as a terrible change in character strikes you as the Sneaky Bob who was there all along, if you had only been shrewd enough to put two and two together after you first heard him talk.

When people express one view, they may be thinking the opposite. They may have said simply what they knew the other person wanted to hear. They may, on second thought, find out that they should have greatly qualified their remarks. They may suddenly regret that they ever spoke out at all. That is why speech, as a way of characterization, moves forward by means of partial concealment, partial exposure. When, however, a writer introduces a man or woman who is to be revealed almost entirely by his or her speech, he will need all his skill to bring that character off. In James's novel *Washington Square*, Mrs. Penniman is just such a character, skillfully brought off. James tells us that she was romantic, sentimental, and that she had an innocent passion for little secrets and mysteries—all of which he manages to demonstrate in just what she says. But most central characters in fiction, like most humans, are more complex.

Speech alone can give clues to a character's origins, background, education, status, and intellect. This is not nearly so precise a matter in America as it is in England, where accent and vocabulary are the immediate marks of class, but Americans have their telltale indications as well. There are such well-recognized differences as that between speech formed at Groton and Harvard and one derived from rural Alabama public schools. More important, there are now special jargons for professions, occupations, and even life-styles. The syntax and vocabulary of a Washington bureaucrat, the speech of a drug dealer in Miami, the words of a computer hacker, the oral style of a women's liberation militant, the expression of a university professor in the liberal arts—all have have their distinctive matrices of speech.

About dialect and bad grammar—they should be avoided except when vital to something in the character or story. Dialect is wearying to read. If the writer needs it for characterization, he should peg it on a few typical expressions or pronunciations. Otherwise, it should be suggested by syntax. Flannery O'Connor was deft at this. She gave the flavor of Southern rural speech by using just a few special words and locutions. Hazel Moats in *Wise Blood* will always say "theter" for "that there [thing]" and a past action is rendered by "done," as in "he done murdered somebody" or "it's done gone." But, otherwise, there are few special effects of grammar or pronunciation. The important point is that we can always hear Haze's nasal, north-Georgia voice in every sentence.

The use of bad grammar can be tricky. It usually denotes a lack of education, but sometimes it may be used by people who know better—or it can be an old-fashioned locution that has fallen out of favor. It is sometimes surprising for Americans to hear an educated Englishman say "The dog et his food," which sounds like rural bad grammar here. "Ain't" began as an English upper-class affectation in the eighteenth century, and there would be a difference between having Lord Cardigan say "ain't" in a novel and having a 1980's Detroit autoworker say it.

A common fault among fiction writers is that of making every character in the book speak the same way. Many authors are open to this sin of omission, so they must consciously vary rhythms, vocabulary, and the length or brevity of speech as much as possible. They must make the style conform as closely as possible to the personality. Certain characteristic expressions can be repeated as part of a pattern of speech, but it is best to use them sparingly.

In this chapter, there was a warning earlier about using dialogue as an information-bearing device. That was not meant as a blanket rule against all discussion of knowledge that people in a story may have in common. Lovers or good friends, say, might have a reason to recall experiences shared in the past—and the reader can learn something from their reminiscent conversation. An inveterate gossip might rattle on to a sympathetic listener about matters perfectly well known to both of them—but now cast in a new light because of some fresh turn of events. People meeting after a long separation often ask each other, "Do you know what's become of ———?" And the answer might begin, "Yes; you remember how she used to. . . ." Speech, properly used, is one of the best methods of building up a sense of characters' pasts, their tastes and motivations, as well as their relationships with one another.

Conversation is never a very good way of reporting action or physical events important to the story. Too often a novice writer will report in talk in order to evade reporting by direct observation—and thereby dulls the edge of the event. After a soldier has come home from combat, say, we hear his experiences as told by his mother to her best friend

—the primary subject, then, is not what he experienced but how his mother responds to the tale of what he experienced. Thus, the occasional exception to this principle will have the purpose of telling a good deal more about the teller than about the event being described.

Speech may serve other purposes besides those outlined in this section, but these, in some combination, are its general principles:

1. It should be brief, because in life we seldom say more than a few sentences at a time.
2. It should add to the reader's present knowledge.
3. It should omit, or quickly pass over, the routine exchanges of ordinary conversation.
4. It should sound spontaneous but avoid the repetitions of real talk.
5. It should keep the story moving forward; it should not be a mere exhibition of the writer's skill with idiomatic dialogue, or of the writer's wit.
6. It should reveal something about the speakers' personalities, both directly and indirectly.
7. It should show relationships among people.

ATTRIBUTION

"Thank you," she exploded. "Tea?" he exclaimed. "I love you, Mavis," expostulated Martin. "Such damn' bloody nonsense!" remarked the general. And, of course, the classic quotation from Ring Lardner: "Shut up," he explained.

The problem of attribution is always there. There is

someone handing that cup of tea and someone breathing next to Mavis' ear—and the writer feels obliged to tell us how that someone's voice sounds. Many writers think that *said* does the job better than any other word because it is neutral and therefore unobtrusive.

"I hate you," she said.

"You don't really," he said. "You hate yourself so much that you think you hate me for trying to help you."

"Just a minute," said Austin as he walked in the door. "How can you hate a priest who's thinking only of your welfare?"

"Easily," she said, "when he's my meddling brother more than he is a priest."

Like the onion in cooking, *said* is a basic ingredient in dialogue. But there can be too much of it, and there are times when it needn't be there at all. In a brief scene between two characters, it is necessary to identify each speaker once only:

"Come down for the weekend," Margaret said.

"Oh, I don't think I could face it," Mrs. Baker said. "Too many memories. Nobody your age understands how painful nostalgia can be."

"Well, I loved him, too, you know. Come, come. It's been ten years and the place is entirely different now."

"I guess I should try. I've got over it, mostly. Strange, isn't it, how mere places can still hurt you after all the years?"

If that passage were to continue for several pages, it would suffice to use an occasional *Margaret said*, or *Mrs. Baker said*, simply as reminders.

Often the *he said/she said* can be left out by indications
such as: Margaret shook her head. "Mother, I think . . ." This
minor activity is what is known in the theater as "business,"
and, while useful to vary scenes of dialogue, it can get too
busy if overdone. And, once the writer moves to a scene with
three or more people, he has to distinguish the voices from
one another by sharp contrasts, or else again rely on the *saids*.

There are a fair number of substitutes for *said,* and they
should almost never be used. They are: exploded, expostulated, ejaculated, hissed, wheezed, chortled, smirked, chuck-
led, growled, groaned, trilled, breathed, croaked, and snarled.
(People can say things *with* a chuckle, a groan, a smirk and
so on.) Then there are those playful inventions of Henry
James that make many of his novels sound like a game of
catch: *She flung at him,* and *He laughingly tossed back.*

After a question, one always uses *he asked* or *he inquired*
but never *said.* (*Queried* is a rare substitute.) *He replied* to or
he answered the question. To offer his opinion, *he observed* or
remarked. When he wished to single out something, *he noted*
or *he pointed out.* Under some exceptional stimulus, he might
cry, cry out, or *shout,* or *yell* or *bellow.* She might *scream.* A
character may sometimes *exclaim, murmur* a comment, or
whisper something. Occasionally, he may *announce* or *declare.*
Now and again, he may *repeat* or *echo* an earlier remark.

In short, the language offers enough reasonable substitutes for *said* to make disconcerting ones unnecessary.

Notes to Chapter 3

1. Garden City, N.Y.: Doubleday & Co., 1941; p. 96.
2. New York: Harcourt, Brace & Co., 1937; p. 179.
3. Boston: Gambit, 1972; p. 156.
4. New York: Charles Scribner's Sons, 1972; p. 51.
5. New York: George H. Doran Co., 1920; p. 131.
6. London: Oxford University Press, 1966; pp. 3–4.
7. New York: Harcourt, Brace & World, 1966; p. 113.
8. "Less is Less," *Harper's Magazine*, April 1986, p. 64.
9. New York: Harcourt, Brace & World, 1966; p. 113.
10. From *Dubliners* (New York: Modern Library, 1927), pp. 281–82.
11. New York: E.P. Dutton, 1961; p. 220.

FOUR

CHARACTERIZATION

John Steinbeck's *In Dubious Battle* has the identities of its characters overwhelmed by the events in which they take part. The book was a popular success because many readers in 1936 were curious about militant labor and its battles against the establishment—just as succeeding generations of readers have wanted to learn about life in the army, the political intrigues on Capitol Hill, the business of high fashion, the history of Hawaii, or the behavior of the Texas rich. But we are no more likely to reread such a novel than we are to settle down for a comfortable evening with the 1910 *World Almanac*. The novel may have something more of a plot, but it will run the almanac a close second for statistical content.

By contrast, we usually find it difficult to recall what a great work of literature was about—unless we say that it was about certain fictional human beings we remember vividly. A half a century ago, Gertrude Stein wrote, "For our purposes, for our contemporary purposes, events have no importance," and she probably had in mind those novels of social realism inspired by the Depression era. There is a kind of irony in her words because once again, in the late years of the century, the novel of event seems to be in the ascendant.

Various theories, none entirely persuasive, have been advanced for the relative decline of character in fiction. Mary McCarthy calls James Joyce "the last great creator of character in the English novel," and she adds, "It is the same on the continent. After Proust, a veil is drawn." Charles Newman, the editor and critic, has noted, "from the contemporary perspective, the contemporary character's one-dimensionality is precisely what is most real about him."

When we try to recall memorable characters, we usually think of people in nineteenth- and early twentieth-century novels. Mary McCarthy believes that the "sense of character began to fade with D. H. Lawrence," and she finds no more than a scattering of striking personalities in more recent fiction, among them: Jason in *The Sound and the Fury*, Studs Lonigan, and Henderson in *Henderson the Rain King*.

The McCarthy essay, written over twenty years ago, still speaks a partial truth about the "fading" of the sense of character, but it is a generalization with many exceptions. There are a numerous examples to show that the art of character-drawing has flourished in the work of good writers in the past two decades. Anthony Powell's long series of related narratives, *A Dance to the Music of Time*, is a joyful noise of people over the years. Any of its readers will have no trouble calling up an image of the awful Widmerpool or the shifty Uncle Giles. Herzog, in Saul Bellow's novel of the same name, is a character very hard to forget. There is, of course, John Updike's fine rendering of the personality of Rabbit Angstrom over the course of three novels. Portnoy in Philip Roth's *Portnoy's Complaint,* Martha Quest in Doris Lessing's *Children of Violence,* Allie Fox in Paul Theroux's *The Mosquito Coast,* and Lore Segal's Ilka Weissnix in *Her First American.* And this is not the end of the list by any means.

E. M. Forster defines "flat" characters as those immediately recognizable because they have habitual forms of expression or habitual responses to any situation. Circumstances do not change them nor do we have to worry about their improving themselves with complications. There are many good ones in the pages of modern writers—ones so immediately recognizable that it is unnecessary to mention the books in which they appear: Bertie Wooster, Nurse Ratchitt, Mrs. Danvers, Sam Spade, Yossarian, Miss Marple, Jocko de Paris, and a host of others. Forster says of them: "They are easily remembered by the reader afterward. They remain in his mind as unalterable for the reason that they were not changed by circumstances, which gives them in retrospect a comforting quality, and preserves them when the book that produced them may decay."

Mary McCarthy argues that the decline in the writer's ability to create complex, fully realized characters comes from the fact that fiction lost interest in watching characters as they behaved in their society, as social creatures.

There came to be two favorite directions—either toward the novel of sensibility (E. M. Forster and Virginia Woolf; in our time, Shirley Hazzard and Elizabeth Taylor) or toward the novel of sensation (Hemingway and Dos Passos; in our time, Robert Stone and Norman Mailer). She says that both tendencies had the same effect—to take characters out of the imme-

diate world of everyday reality, ruled by mundane obligations, and to put them into very special worlds created for the
sake of the story. An example of the first might be the story
of a woman speaking to her psychiatrist and probing all of her
past and present anxieties, and an example of the second
might be a novel of intrigue or espionage that takes place in
a melodramatic world of plots and conflict. These two tendencies, according to Mary McCarthy, are the poles of each other,
and both have the effect of abolishing the social milieu in
which we are accustomed to making assessments of people
and thus annihilating the sense of character.

McCarthy does leave what she calls "a curious back
door" by which a writer enters into characters of a three-
dimensional kind. The writer shows his characters "inside
out, from behind the screen of consciousness. The interior
monologue every human being conducts with himself, sotto
voce, is used to create a dramatic portrait. In effect, the writer
becomes a sort of ventriloquist, impersonating his characters
rather than presenting them from the outside."

Except by way of that back door, according to McCarthy,
the writer has lost the power "to speak in his own voice or
through the undisguised voice of an alter ego."

Whether or not these gloomy misgivings apply to all
present-day fiction, the main points are true. A character is
fully realized only when he or she acts within a social context,
and no serious work of fiction can succeed without at least one
fully realized character at its heart.

Two traditional ways of presenting characters are by
means of an introductory portrait or by means of a portrait
that develops slowly and subtly throughout the novel. The
first has the simple merit of establishing a character in the

reader's mind at the outset. The second is more lifelike in that it imitates our daily experience—we get to know people little by little and our understanding of them is built up through many small encounters and observations. Here is a rather old-fashioned example of the first method from Thomas Hardy's *Jude the Obscure:*

Jude would now have been described as a young man with a forcible, meditative, an earnest rather than handsome cast of countenance. He was of dark complexion, with dark, harmonizing eyes, and he wore a closely-trimmed black beard of more advanced growth than is usual at his age; this, with his great mass of curly black hair, was some trouble to him in combing and washing out the stone-dust that settled on it in the pursuit of his trade.[1]

Here is a deft example of the same method from a recent novel, Patricia Chute's *Eva's Music:*

I paced my little balcony. It was easy to picture Cal, angular, breezy, his hair flopping over his forehead, full of smiles, which I knew covered a touch of melancholy, a hint of self-doubt. He helped me carry my harp so many times, in and out of the elevator, into the car, down the stairs; "Worse than an eight-man shell," he grumbled. My fun Cal, whom I curled up with, our legs looped over each other, as recently as a month ago, whom I had driven to the dentist to have a wisdom tooth out a mere two weeks ago, who claimed, occasionally, to love me. . . .[2]

Such introductory capsule characterizations are rare in serious fiction today, although they are still common in popular fiction. Earlier writers knew quite well that they were using a literary device when putting their characters in full view at the beginning of the story. It was not lifelike; it was —to use a theatrical term—a matter of casting. Heroine, hero, villain, and comedy relief were quickly defined. In life, it takes time to discover who, if anyone, is a hero, what woman will join with him as wife or lover, who will emerge to complicate their relationship.

One reason for the decline of capsule characterization is probably the decline of the old-fashioned plot with all its obligations. There role responsibilities had to be assigned early in order to set the mechanism going without question marks about any of the people.

It is often said that characters must "grow and change in the course of the novel," but we know that many people in real life remain basically unchanged after they reach maturity. They "grow and change" only in the sense that we get to know them better and better. Over the course of a friendship, or over the course of a novel, we gradually realize the complex reasons behind their characteristic behavior patterns. Quite early we noticed that Karen seemed to shun and dislike children. She never changed, but later on, we understood her a little better when we found out that she had once been a battered child.

A good example of first impressions confirmed and deepened appears in Edith Wharton's *The Custom of the Country*. At the outset, Undine Spragg appears as a selfish, imperious girl. As the story goes on, it becomes plain that these traits spring from a nature that is amoral, coldhearted, self-indulgent, ambitious, and—as it affects other people—evil.

Henry James wrote a famous essay called "The Art of

Fiction" in which he asked, "What is character but the deter-
mination of incident? What is incident but the illustration of
character?" Many stories and novels move forward by showing how the traits first noticed in the protagonist bring about
events that he is not able to control. These events are going
to leave their mark on him, and what he has learned (or failed
to learn) about himself has also deepened the reader's understanding of him.

In Sinclair Lewis's *Babbitt*, George Babbitt, bored with
his current life, gets involved with Tanis Judique, her bohe-
mian friends, and their liberal causes—and scandalizes his
conservative business friends. Although he eventually reverts
to type, the experience of the love affair and the excursion
into liberalism have tempered his stereotyped views of the
world. When his son rebels against convention, Babbitt understands and supports him—a course that would have been
impossible for the stuffy, middle-American George we met at
the beginning of the story.

This is a clear-cut example of the way an author can
produce changes of outlook and conduct over a space of
fictional time, but it is not a very subtle or skillful one. Babbitt
is first one thing, then another, and finally a mixture of both.
There is a discontinuity to his image. Characters should display a certain consistency, even though they are subject to
change. But that consistency should not prevent them from
surprising us now and then. A new circumstance may produce
some buried impulse, or some long-pent-up emotion may
come out in action or speech. It is then the writer's job to
convince his reader that what may have seemed shockingly

out of character at the moment was really both intelligible and inevitable.

To sum up, these distinctions would finally yield four different character-drawing methods:

The first would be that of the changeless character (e.g., the woman who is totally directed toward some end, or the hero-detective in a crime novel).

The second would be that of the one-change character. (The innocent, trusting girl who arrives in the big city and becomes hardened and cynical.)

The third would be the changeless but more complicated character, not fully known to us early on but gradually "unrolled" in the course of the book. (Jay Gatsby in *The Great Gatsby.*)

The fourth would be the character who is gradually revealed or "unrolled" but who also changes in temperament or outlook as circumstances affect him. (Raskolnikov in *Crime and Punishment.*)

All four of these methods have their uses according to whatever sort of story the author has decided to tell. But, from an aesthetic viewpoint, the last method is the finest accomplishment. It produces a many-sided character whom we get to know in encounter after encounter—the refreshing thing being that she or he surprises us a little each time. And we are also observing this emerging person being changed by the events of life. It is, of course, much more than a great technical feat; it is the center of the art of the novel.

Once the writer has decided on the method by which he is going to present his characters, he must decide on the best techniques for making them into flesh and blood for the reader. He will want to use some or all of the following:

1. Physical appearance.
2. Movements, expressions, mannerisms, habits.
3. Behavior toward others.
4. Speech.
5. Attitude toward self.
6. Attitude of others toward the character.
7. Physical surroundings.
8. Past.
9. Fringe techniques such as names and figures of speech.

These are the conventional methods of characterization. Modern writers have often employed the stream-of-consciousness technique, which will be discussed in a separate section of this chapter.

PHYSICAL APPEARANCE

Nineteenth-century writers were lavish with detail, and they could scarcely let a character go without describing him from his widow's peak and Roman nose, down through his neckcloth, coat, waistcoat, and faultless breeches, to his exquisitely polished boots. Here is Benjamin Disraeli describing a character in *Coningsby:*

He . . . was a man of middle size and age, originally in all probability of a spare habit, but now a little inclined to corpulency. Baldness, perhaps, contributed to the spiritual expression of a brow which was, however, essentially intellectual, and gave some character of openness to a countenance which, though not ill-favoured, was unhappily stamped with a sinister cast that was not to be mistaken. His manner was easy, but rather audacious than well-bred.

Indeed, while a visage which might otherwise be described as handsome was spoiled by a dishonest glance, so a demeanour that was by no means deficient in self-possession and facility, was tainted by an innate vulgarity, which in the long run, though seldom, yet surely developed itself.[3]

This is a useful passage to look at because everything is wrong with it. To begin with, a reader can't hold so many rather vague details in his mind if they are packed together this way. In trying to produce an image, the writer has given a succession of small images that do not cohere to make a portrait. How big and how old is a man of "middle size and middle age"? Try to imagine a face with a forehead that seems to be spiritual but is actually intellectual. How do we know that the man is "innately vulgar"? What makes a glance dishonest? A physical description made up of such clichés and generalities will never convey any clear picture to the reader.

Coningsby came out in 1844. It would be unfair to imply that all writers of the period handled portraiture as badly as Disraeli did. Here is a passage from Sheridan Le Fanu's *Uncle Silas:*

Mr. Bryerly arrived in time enough to dress at his leisure, before dinner. He entered the drawing room—a tall, lean man, all in ungainly black, with a white choker, with either a black wig or black hair dressed in imitation of one, a pair of spectacles, and a dark, sharp, short, visage, rubbing his large hands together, and with a short, brisk nod to me, whom he plainly regarded merely as a child, he sat down before the fire, crossed his legs, and took up a magazine.[4]

The difference is that Disraeli never really saw his man but Le Fanu saw his, stepping very lifelike into that drawing room, sitting down by the fire, and giving just a hint of trouble.

As the century moved on, writers learned to use their drawing instruments with more sophistication. Following are two excerpts from Robert Louis Stevenson's *Treasure Island:*

> I remember him as if it were yesterday, as he came plodding up to the inn door, his sea-chest following him in a hand-barrow; a tall, strong, heavy, nut-brown man; his tarry pigtail falling over the shoulders of his soiled blue coat; his hands ragged and scarred, with black, broken nails; and the sabre cut across one cheek, a dirty, vivid white.
>
> •   •   •
>
> His left leg was cut off close by the hip, and under the left shoulder he carried a crutch, which he managed with wonderful dexterity, hopping about upon it like a bird. He was very tall and strong, with a face as big as a ham—plain and pale but intelligent and smiling. Indeed, he seemed in the most cheerful spirits, whistling as he moved about among the tables, with a merry word or a slap on the shoulder for the most favored of his guests.[5]

Stevenson had mastered the art of the one-minute sketch that caught the shape of things and a few highlights—the dirty white scar shining in a dark brown face, the huge cripple hopping with his crutch, light as a bird. The point to note about his descriptions is that they are made on the move. The sea dog in the blue coat plods up to the inn door. In a moment, he will rap with his stick and demand a glass of rum. We have observed him very clearly, though the story has not paused for an instant, and we have not been aware of a writer at work on a portrait.

Here is a more static example, from a modern work (Muriel Spark's *The Comforters*):

> At seventy-eight, Louisa Jepp did everything very slowly, but with extreme attention, as some do when they know they are slightly drunk. . . .
> Louisa's hair is black, though there is not much of it. She is short, and seen from the side especially, her form resembles a neat double potato just turned up from the soil with its small round head, its body from which hang the roots, her two thin legs below her full brown skirt and corpulence.[6]

"Neat double potato" is the telling metaphoric detail here—but no physical characteristic should be put in simply because it is immediately eye-catching. The looks and traits pointed out in the original description have to be genuine aspects of the character as we get to know him or her. If there is to be nothing vegetable-like and earthy about Louisa Jepp's personality, we have been the victims of a small fraud.

Most serious writers use physical detail straightforwardly as one means of making their people appear real. But now and again a writer will use one of the stock figures of fiction—the dear little old lady, the dashing rogue, the jolly fat man—as a deception. Having aroused the usual expectations that go with the type, the writer then shows the character to be something entirely different. It is not good practice.

No character in serious fiction should be a total stereotype, first of all, and then no description should be used merely as a way to hoodwink the reader. William Faulkner does this rather shamelessly in his famous story, "A Rose for Emily." Miss Emily is all those things we expect a Southern lady of reduced fortunes to be. As a girl, after a long illness, she had "a vague resemblance to those angels in colored church windows—sort of tragic and serene." In her thirties, she was "still a slight woman . . . with cold, haughty black eyes in a face the flesh of which was strained across the temples and about the eyesockets as you imagine a lighthouse keeper's face ought to look." In old age, she became "a small, fat woman in black, with a thin gold chain descending to her waist and vanishing into her belt, leaning on an ebony cane with a tarnished gold head." The great sorrow in Miss Emily's life has been a long-ago desertion by her dashing suitor.

After she finally dies and people enter her bedroom, they find a skeleton on one side of the bed—that of Miss Emily's faithless suitor whom she had murdered years before—and on the other side, a pillow with "the indentation of a head," and from this hollow, one of the party lifts "a long strand of iron-gray hair." And William Faulkner has been caught impersonating a combination of Mary Roberts Rinehart and Edgar Allan Poe.

MOVEMENTS, EXPRESSIONS, MANNERISMS, AND HABITS

"Each time he found some item of particular interest, he called Mrs. Flagg and she came over, moving cheerfully and quickly like a farmer's wife at a square dance." This sentence, from Leslie Thomas's *The Love Beach*, captures neatly and amusingly the suggestion of a quick and cheerful nature. In *Too Much of Water,* Bruce Hamilton introduces a man who sits in the dining saloon of a cruise ship: "He dived instantly into the menu, rather in the manner of a hen investigating her feathers, so that almost all immediately visible of him was a satisfyingly bald head." These minor actions are effective because they illustrate an aspect of character, but beginning writers are often guilty of inserting insignificant actions just in order to break up the dialogue. Many cigarettes have been lighted, many noses rubbed, many throats cleared in that endeavor.

Movements and gestures should be integral to the action of the fiction, as well as illustrative of character. Someone may get up to peer through a window; she may get out of one chair and sit down in another; she may leave the room to fix herself a drink. But, when she makes these small moves, the reader must say to himself, "I see that she doesn't miss a thing that goes on next door," or "Every conversation seems to bore her so that she can't sit still" or "Oops, that's the fourth drink in an hour—something's going to happen."

Mannerisms and habits, if not used carefully, can come to irritate a reader. As noted earlier, they are often used as tags for the easy identification of flat characters, but they can get wearisome when the characters are supposed to be more fully realized. In *Jane and Prudence,* Barbara Pym introduces Jane, a vicar's wife who is an inept housekeeper, a worse cook, and a social embarrassment because of her habit of speaking out when common sense should have told her to shut up. As H. G. Wells once remarked of the novelist "Elizabeth," if you'd known her for a week, you'd want to bang her head against the wall. It takes less time for Jane to arouse that impulse in the reader.

An especially effective use of mannerism or habit is to show something that belies a character's ostensible attitude and brings out what he is really feeling or thinking. It is like the involuntary tic of an eyelid. "His attentive face relaxed a little. But I saw one of his feet, softly, quietly, incessantly beating on the carpet under the table"—a passage from Wilkie Collins's *The Woman in White.* The lady who protests too much, the smiler with the knife, the clown who is inwardly weeping—all are familiar figures. When someone's manner seems forced, look for a giveaway sign elsewhere, and the character's real state of mind will be dramatized in the contradiction.

A very complex example of revealing gesture is Ernest Hemingway's story "Big Two-Hearted River." The story is entirely made up of Nick Adams's thoughts and gestures. We usually think of gesture as something observed by others; in this case, Nick Adams is all alone in the woods and is not—consciously or unconsciously—trying to communicate anything. We, the readers, are the only observers, playing the game of trying to single out the significant motions among all the quite ordinary ones of making camp and fishing the river. The significant gestures will tell us what is going on under the surface of Nick's mind.

One way to use mannerisms effectively is by showing some action, gesture, stance, bodily attitude, or change of aspect that betrays hidden emotion in a character. Eighteenth-century fiction writers were not very good observers of this (see Defoe or Fielding), but writers of the following

century began to associate certain physical manifestations
with certain emotions. In their books, ladies color when they
are surprised or embarrassed. Men stiffen and turn pale when
they are angry; people hang their heads in shame, cast their
eyes down if they are shy, curl their lips in disdain, or frown
in deep thought. These are visual clichés that, like all clichés,
often have some validity.

Becoming a little more elaborate about it, Charlotte
Brontë (in *Jane Eyre*) wrote: "He gave my wrist a convulsive
grip; the smile on his lips froze; apparently a spasm caught
his breath." By the early twentieth century, writers were
trying to read quite complicated emotions in the expression
of a face or the movements of a body. But it was not until the
1950s that systematic studies of "nonverbal communication"
were undertaken by a combination of psychologists, an-
thropologists, and sociologists.

One of the early investigators, Ray Birdwhistell, has said
that his studies show that meaning in any social exchange is
about 35 percent verbal and 65 percent nonverbal. This is an
astonishing estimate. It suggests that our tics, our eye engage-
ment, our manner of sitting, the distance we preserve between
ourselves and others, the way we move our hands, our hesita-
tions in speech, and a hundred other things are more eloquent
expressions of what we mean than any words we might use.

This is a matter of extreme importance to writers, most
of whom have never bothered to become more than casual
observers of the silent language communicated by the body.
Take the face, for example.

Writers have always used it as the primary register of
emotions—and yet it is frequently the most unreliable of any.

Paul Ekman, in his *Emotion in the Human Face,* analyzed half a century of research and concluded that sometimes basic human emotions are very clearly shown in the face—but these times are likely to be in the bedroom, the kitchen, or the bathroom. It is anatomically possible to display over a thousand different facial expressions. There can be mixed expressions (smiling mouth but angry eyes), deceptive expressions (a poker face), or associative expressions (when, say, one part of the face shows bafflement and another shows insecurity.)

The eyes are usually thought to be the most expressive part of the face—"the eyes are the mirror of the soul"—and some writers tend to overinterpret them, finding some very complicated ideas and emotions in whites and pupils. The important thing to notice, however, is the way people use their eyes. Among Americans, there are certain set rituals about eye contact. Staring is rude; strangers in an elevator avoid eye contact; when strangers approach each other on a street, eye contact is broken off at a distance of about eight feet; a speaker keeps up intermittent eye contact and his listener maintains a steady gaze as a sign of interest; in conversation, a superior tends to break off eye contact while the inferior tries to hold it; a waiter avoids eye contact when he intends to ignore you; and so on.

Eye customs can be deceptive, however, because they differ so much among various cultures. Arabs, when they talk, tend to stand close and look intently into each others' eyes —a stance reserved for lovers in America. In Hispanic culture, a well-bred young woman avoids eye contact with a man —which is often considered a sign of lying or deception in

America. In Israel, people tend to stare at one another in public; in the Orient, staring is considered rude.

Bodily postures are clues both to character and attitude. A judge on the bench leans forward with an intent expression while the prosecution is pleading and reclines far back in his chair while the defense has the floor—and his sympathies are evident. (This was actually observed in a famous trial in the 1960s.) While she is telling a story about her aggressive, intimidating boss, a young woman folds her arms across her chest—a typically defensive gesture. A banker makes a steeple of his fingers while listening to a client appeal for a loan —he has a feeling of superiority and his hands show it. There are hundreds of other physical attitudes closely associated with mental attitudes. But do people ordinarily pick up such signals? According to the researchers, we all have an intuitive grasp of them and, subconsciously, we factor them into the total encounter.

There is a whole series of cues that have been classified as courting behaviors. "Palming" is one of them. Most American or English women tend to keep their fingers curled, seldom showing anything of their palms. When women are in a courting encounter, however, they tend to show their palms freely. Other courtship gestures are preening, standing close, exchanging long looks, surrogate touching, and so on. Often these are not sexual signals at all—even though they mimic the courtship attitudes—and they can take place between parent and child, doctor and patient, student and teacher, in fact between any people who have established a rapport of whatever kind.

This is no more than a hint of all the fascinating literature about nonverbal communication. Writers would do well to read some of it and to learn to observe with that knowledge in mind. The understanding of character and the interaction between characters is dependent on interpretation of the unspoken to such an extent that the success of a novel may depend on the success of that interpretation. Characters who possess voices only may strike the reader as talking heads.

BEHAVIOR TOWARD OTHERS

In one of his stories, Maupassant introduces a big man with a red beard who always went first through a door. It is an instant portrait of confidence, even a certain arrogance, and it is all that is necessary to give the reader a definite impression of that man.

A different and more extended example comes from a story of John Cheever's titled "The Cure." The narrator, separated from his wife and living alone, comes to believe that someone is spying on him through his windows at night. One morning, after such an incident, he goes to the railway station to look for the intruder:

Even though I had only seen the face dimly, I thought that I would recognize it. Then I saw my man. It was as simple as that. He was waiting on the platform for the eight-ten with the rest of us, but he wasn't any stranger.

It was Herbert Marston, who lives in the big yellow house on Blenhollow Road. If there had been any question in my mind, it would have been answered by the way he looked when he saw that I recognized him. He looked frightened and guilty. I started across the platform to speak to him. "I don't mind you looking in my windows at night, Mr. Marston," I was going to say in a voice loud enough to embarrass him, "but I wish that you wouldn't trample on my wife's flowers." Then I stopped because I saw that he was not alone. He was with his wife and daughter. . . .

There was nothing irregular in Mr. Marston's features or—when he saw that I was going to leave him alone—in his manner. . . . The belief that a crooked heart is betrayed by palsies, tics, and other infirmities dies hard. I felt the loss of it that morning when I searched his face for some mark.[7]

This is a nicely complicated example because we do not perceive any sign of guilt in Marston but we watch the narrator perceive one. Cheever has directed our attention to Marston for telltale signs in his manner, but what starts to dawn on us is that the narrator's behavior is beginning to seem the peculiar one.

The narrator looks at Marston's very pretty daughter and at Mrs. Marston's face. "Her face was sallow and plain, but it was wreathed, even while she watched for the morning train, in an impermeable smile. It was a face that must have seemed long ago cut out for violent, even malevolent, passion. But years of prayer and abstinence had expunged the inclination to violence. . . . She must pray for him, I thought, while he wanders around backyards in his bathrobe."

With that perfectly unwarranted interpretation on the narrator's part, we reach the suspicion that the attitude that we should be paying attention to is not Marston's but the narrator's—here is, in fact, a case of paranoia. Not only paranoia but, perhaps, transference, because we have previously been told how unforgiving the narrator is toward his own wife.

Behavior toward others will not necessarily be as pronounced a case as this. In Henry James's *The Portrait of a Lady,* Isabel Archer observes Gilbert Osmond sitting and the sinister Madame Merle standing as they talk. By this fact alone, Isabel detects a very subtle sign that the two have been lovers. This would be lost on the modern reader—probably even on some contemporary readers—if James had not come forward to tell us what it meant.

SPEECH

Because speech is the subject of an earlier chapter, it will be treated briefly here. A fundamental principle of fiction is that each character of any importance in the story should express his personality in what he says: individualism comes out in rhythms, locutions, idioms, peculiarities, brevity or long-windedness, and syntax. To say that Huck Finn does not speak like Stephen Dedalus is to put it as drastically as possible. The writer should constantly ask himself whether this is how she or he would say this thing. Are the words typical?

Here is a bad example from *The Old Man and the Sea:*

"You were nearly killed [says the old man] when I brought the fish in too green and he nearly tore the boat to pieces. Can you remember?"

"I can remember [the boy replies] the tail slapping and banging and the thwart breaking and the noise of the clubbing. I can remember you throwing me into the bow where the wet coiled lines were and feeling the whole boat shiver and the noise of you clubbing him like chopping a tree down and the sweet blood smell all over me."[8]

What is wrong with this reply? It is too "literary," too detailed and too precise. The reader has stopped hearing the fisher boy and is listening instead to the author, who has lost touch with his character. The boy is of course capable of the impressions but not of voicing them in Ernest Hemingway's style. Experience and oral expression have been divorced.

Here is a good example of an individual style—that of Paul Theroux's Allie Fox, the father in *The Mosquito Coast*. Allie is a knowledgable crank and a nonstop theorizer. He is shopping:

"Let me see some knapsacks [Father said]. If they're from Japan, you can keep them."

"These are Chinese—People's Republic. You wouldn't be interested" [the salesman replied].

"Give us here," Father said, and holding the little green knapsack like a rag he turned to Clover. "A few years ago we were practically at war with the People's Republic. Red Chinese we called them. Reds. Slants. Gooks. Ask anyone. Now they're selling us knapsacks—probably for the next war. What's the catch? They're third-rate knapsacks, they wouldn't hold sandwiches. You think we're going to win that war against the Chinese?"[9]

Few characters will be as full of eccentric ego as Allie, but even with more subdued leading characters, the writer should constantly keep in mind the thought that speech is not only concerned with the exchange of information but also with the characters' attitudes, origins, education, sensitivity, and intelligence as well as the verbal attributes listed at the beginning of this section.

ATTITUDE TOWARD SELF

Most women and men like to believe that the rest of the world sees them as they choose to be seen, in the role they have decided to play. It is usually a role that displays the characteristics they think of as their best. Probably there are people in the world whose self-evaluation is accepted by everyone around them, but these people should not find their way into fiction. There must be drama of some sort in the encounter of characters. But prior to that comes a character's self-appraisal. That self-appraisal can fall anywhere in the range from neurotic introspection to total unselfconsciousness, but the reader must learn it in order to know what the character's words and actions mean—in the slang phrase, "where he's coming from."

In Giuseppe di Lampedusa's small masterpiece, *The Leopard*, Prince Fabrizio often examines himself, sometimes with wisdom, sometimes with the blinders of his caste and politics and—in this case—with a revealing touch of hypocrisy. After dinner one night, he has suddenly decided to drive into Palermo despite the obvious distress of his wife, Stella. He is going to visit his mistress:

"I'm a sinner, I know, doubly a sinner by Divine Law and by Stella's human love. There's no doubt of that and tomorrow I'll go and confess to Father Pirrone." . . . And then a spirit of quibble came over him again. "I'm sinning, it's true, but I'm sinning so as not to sin worse, to stop this sensual nagging, to tear this thorn out of my flesh and avoid worse trouble. That the Lord knows." Suddenly he was swept by a gust of tenderness toward himself. "I'm just a poor, weak creature," he thought as his heavy steps crunched the dirty gravel. "I'm weak and without support. Stella! Oh well, the Lord knows how much I've loved her; but I was married at twenty. And now she's too bossy as well as too old." His moment of weakness passed. "But I've still got my vigor; and how can I find satisfaction with a woman who makes the sign of the Cross in bed before every embrace and then at the crucial moment just cries 'Gesummaria!' When we married and she was sixteen, I found that rather exalting; but now . . . seven children I've had with her, seven; and never once have I seen her navel. Is that right?" Now, whipped by this odd anguish, he was almost shouting, "It is right? I ask you all!" and he turned to the portico of the Catena. "Why, she's the real sinner!"

Comforted by this reassuring discovery, he gave a firm knock at Mariannina's door.

In another moment of insight, the prince makes a better impression:

Flattery always slipped off the Prince like water off the leaves of water lilies: it is one of the advantages enjoyed by men who are at once proud and used to being so. "This fellow here seems to be under the impression that he's come to do me a great honor," he was thinking. "To me, who am what I am, among other things a Peer of the Kingdom of Sicily. . . . It's true that one must value gifts in relation to those who offer them; when a peasant gives me his bit of cheese, he's making me a bigger present than the Prince of

Lascari when he invites me to dinner. That's obvious. The difficulty is that the cheese is nauseating. So all that remains is the heart's gratitude, which can't be seen, and the nose wrinkled in disgust, which can be seen only too well."[10]

Largely by such insights, the portrait of the prince becomes vivid, elaborate, and convincing. And largely through them is his character "unrolled" to a point where we can—almost—predict how he will act and react.

There should be some mention of the use of the mirror in fiction. It is one of the most ubiquitous of props. Authors have their characters look into mirrors so that we can see what they look like without being told directly. Along with that, we get an idea of how the character looks at himself. Mignon Eberhart, the mystery writer, a dab hand at mirrors, introduces this passage into *Hasty Wedding:*

She paused at the dressing table; sat down and leaned forward to look at herself in the mirror. There might have been times when she could have thanked the Lord for a straight nose and fine skin and lovely, deep eye sockets. For deep blue eyes and a gay smile. For a soft masking of the firm Whipple chin. For glancing, evanescent moments of spiritual beauty. But it was not one of those times. She was pale and tired and lifeless looking. Beautiful bride indeed![11]

There is nothing inherently wrong with the mirror device except that it has been used so often it is a bit tarnished. It should be avoided unless there is no other device that will do as well.

ATTITUDE OF OTHERS TOWARD THE CHARACTER

There is no accounting for tastes, and the image others have of one may be friendly or unfriendly, generous or censorious —even as no more than the subject of an amusing anecdote. If Mrs. Cross says that Mr. Zero is a snob, it may tell us something about Zero. On the other hand, look closer, the author might actually be telling us something about Mrs. Cross instead. A story by Aldous Huxley called "Nuns at Luncheon" does both. Two old acquaintances—neither of them nuns—meet now and then to gossip and have lunch. There are the male narrator and Miss Penny, "the well-known woman journalist." Today she reports on her "marvelous nun"—a young woman whose tragedy she unearthed while recovering from an operation in a German hospital. The nun's story occupies most of the narrative, but Huxley's real subject is the attitude of the two people at lunch.

In brief, Sister Agatha fell in love with Kuno, a patient at the hospital who was to be "taken back to jail as soon as he could stand firmly on his legs." Kuno persuades the girl to help him escape, takes her with him, rapes her in a shepherd's hut, and then deserts her. Sister Agatha returns to her order, is given symbolic funeral rites, and then becomes a charwoman at the hospital.

This shocking and tragic story is not that at all to Miss Penny and, perhaps, the narrator as well. The reader sees the nun from Penny's point of view and Penny from the narrator's.

Miss Penny thinks she is a femme fatale. At the beginning of the meal, she remarks that she has just escaped the amorous intentions of a Russian general who said that her eyes drove him mad. The narrator comments mentally that Penny has "eyes like a hare's, flush with her head and very bright with a superficial and expressionless brightness. What a formidable woman. I felt sorry for the Russian general."[12]

Miss Penny's interruptions during her tale of the nun are noteworthy. She describes the nun's appearance after her return this way: "She looked as though she were dead. A walking corpse, that's what she was. . . . I shouldn't have thought it possible for anyone to change so much in so short a time. . . . And the general expression of unhappiness—that was something quite appalling."

Those would seem to be compassionate sentiments, but suddenly Miss Penny's mind is on more important things: "She leaned out into the gangway between the two tables and caught the passing waiter by the end of one of his coat-tails. 'Half a pint of Guinness,' ordered Miss Penny."

She's a heartless, garrulous woman in the narrator's account, but that account is also something of a revelation of him. Implicit in the story is what Penny thinks of her friend. Few people tell dirty jokes to their mothers. Not many explain their beliefs about the shiftlessness of the poor to a man who is out of work. Stories are generally reserved for sympathetic audiences, and it is fair to infer that Penny thinks her friend much like herself—not someone who would listen to the hilarious tale of the nun's undoing with a long face.

Not every fiction makes such sophisticated play with attitudes, but the writer must constantly be concerned with revelation of someone's character through attitude.

PHYSICAL SURROUNDINGS

The subject of place or setting is treated in a later chapter, but its use as a method of characterization belongs here. In the past, many writers put as much emphasis on surroundings as they did on physical appearances. The reader was expected to grasp the telling detail of mansion or tenement or farmhouse and to conclude something about the inhabitants.

Dickens took great joy in this idea. Wemmick's house in *Great Expectations* is a little imitation castle with drawbridge, turret, Gothic windows and a flagstaff. Close to it is a "separate fortress constructed of lattice-work" in which is the gun he fires every night at sundown. He loves to sit and smoke his pipe in a bower beside a little ornamental lake. Everything is romantic, domestic, contented—and defensive —in harmony with his character. Miss Havisham's mansion, Satis House, has dark corridors, steep stairs, shrouded windows, dust, cobwebs, rats, and a huge, decaying wedding cake. It all reflects Miss Havisham's ruined life.

In George Eliot's *Middlemarch*, Dorothea Brooke, about to be married, visits Lowick Manor and is shown a room she is to have:

The bow-window looked down the avenue of limes; the furniture was all of a faded blue, and there were miniatures of ladies and gentlemen with powdered hair hanging in a group. A piece of tapestry over a door also showed a blue-green world with a pale stag in it. The chairs and tables were thin-legged and easy to upset. It was a room where one might fancy the ghost of a tight-laced lady revisiting the scene of her embroidery. A light bookcase contained duodecimo volumes of polite literature in calf, completing the furniture.[13]

The room seems to hint quite a lot about the life Dorothea can look forward to after her marriage. Her uncle suggests that she might want to change the furnishings, but she answers that she likes things as they are.

George Eliot is usually no interior decorator, and thus the room so carefully described must be there for a purpose. Is it because Dorothea is a character well-expressed by pale blues, thin-legged tables, and polite literature? Not at all; it is because she is completely indifferent to her surroundings, whatever they may be. She is a cerebral woman, and this small episode about the bow-windowed room reinforces that for us.

The French naturalist writers of the late nineteenth century and their English and American descendants tended to think of people as the product of their environments, the sum of how and where they lived. In reaction to this kind of writing, Willa Cather published her essay, "The Novel Demeublé" in 1922. She wrote, "The elder Dumas enunciated a great principle when he said that to make a drama, a man needed one passion and four walls." The story or novel stripped of excessive furnishings was also the subject of Virginia Woolf's essay "Mr. Bennett and Mrs. Brown" in 1924: "Here is the British public sitting by the writer's side and saying in its vast and unanimous way, 'Old women have houses. They have fathers. They have incomes. They have servants. They have hot water bottles. That is how we know they are old women. Mr. Wells and Mr. Bennett and Mr. Galsworthy have always taught us that this is the way to recognise them.' "

This by no means discouraged the naturalistic writers, and they produced some very good novels in their genre during the 1930s (*The Grapes of Wrath* being a notable example), but naturalistic fiction finally exhausted itself with descriptions of truck stops, public toilets, ramshackle houses on mean streets in the rain, and factories belching soot.

One useful way of presenting physical surroundings is to make them seem almost part of a character's feelings—the kind of anthropomorphism we are all guilty of at times. The character's emotions and the scene are mingled. In Thomas Mann's "Death in Venice," the writer Gustave von Aschenbach takes a long walk through the city while struggling with his secret passion for a beautiful boy and his guilt feelings. He feels oppressed:

There was a hateful sultriness in the narrow streets. The air was so heavy that all the manifold smells wafted out of the houses, shops, and cook-shops—smells of oil, perfumery and so forth—hung low like exhalations, not dissipating. Cigarette smoke seemed to stand in the air, it drifted so slowly away. . . . The longer he walked, the more he was in torture from that state, which is the product of the sea air and the sirocco and which excites and enervates at once. . . . He fled from the huddled, narrow streets of the commercial city, crossed many bridges, and came into the poor quarter of Venice. Beggars waylaid him, the canals sickened him with their evil exhalations.[14]

THE PAST

Edith Wharton once queried Henry James about a novel of his, saying: "What was your idea in suspending the four principal characters in the void? What sort of life did they lead when they were not watching each other and fencing [verbally] with each other? Why have you stripped them of the human fringes we necessarily trail after us through life?" The past, of course, is one of the great "human fringes" we carry, and novice writers usually make one of two mistakes in furnishing their characters with it, providing either too much or too little.

The writer with too much to say can swamp the narrative with memories and memorabilia, but that shows at least that the writer has a robust conception of his characters; he knows "all" about them.

Imagine the protagonist of an imaginary novel. She had a good father and mother whose marriage was close to perfect until her father died when she was twelve. She had twin brothers. In the summer, the family would leave the city and go to her uncle's ranch in Wyoming, where she had a horse. She loved the West. Her best friend was a very intelligent girl whom everybody else laughed at because she had a harelip. In school, she was a good biology student and she learned to play the flute. She was thought to be less bright and less attractive than her brothers; they tolerated her like a good but homely pet. When she was sixteen, she fell madly in love with a track star for six months and lost her virginity. She wanted to go to Bennington, but her mother made her go to Smith. Say that we come upon her in the novel, much later,

trying to paste the pieces back together after a totally disastrous marriage. What facts from her past are going to be the
significant ones relating to her present self and situation?

Characters in fiction ought to have names; they ought to
come from somewhere; they ought to have formative pasts.
The appeal of much Southern writing has lain in a strong
sense of the way the past influences the decisions and actions
of the present. Continuity and change are the basic elements
of life. They give to any story reassurance and suspense. As
G. K. Chesterton said: "We all live in the past because there
is nothing else to live in. To live in the present is like propos-
ing to sit on a pin. It is too minute, too slight a support, it
is too uncomfortable a posture, and it is of necessity followed
immediately by totally different experiences, analogous to
those of jumping up with a yell." This could be a description
of one of the fashionable minimalist stories of the 1980s,
written in the present tense, with almost no past background,
nervous, often jumping up with a yell.

FRINGE TECHNIQUES

In a *New Yorker* staff memorandum, Wolcott Gibbs once
wrote: "Funny names belong to the past. . . . Any character
called Mrs. Middlebottom or Joe Zilch should summarily be
changed to something else." Many writers, nevertheless, have
a weakness for exotic or outrageous names. A Nikolai Gogol
story would never have gotten past Mr. Gibbs into the *New
Yorker*—Gogol was fond of such zingers as the troika driver
Grigory Doyezhai-ne-doye-desh ("drive to where you won't

get"), Madame Korobochka ("little box"), and Akaky Akakyevitch, hero of "The Overcoat."

Edith Wharton, too, would have been banned from the *New Yorker* for such offenses as Undine Spragg, Laura Testvalley, and the worst crime of all, Amalasthuna degli Duchidi Lucera (in *Twilight Sleep*). And Fielding, Dickens, Thackeray, and Evelyn Waugh would never have a chance.

Gibbs's stricture is reasonable enough for serious fiction, although there is an old device of using names to imply personality. There is Mr. Allworthy in *Tom Jones*, the Veneerings in *Our Mutual Friend*, Dobbin in *Vanity Fair*, and Stephen Dedalus in *A Portrait of the Artist as a Young Man*. There is Roger Chillingsworth in *The Scarlet Letter* and Christopher Newman in *The American*.

Despite Gibbs, people have gone on using comic names for comic characterization. The most outrageous inventor was P. G. Wodehouse with such as Rollo Podmarsh, Aunt Dahlia, Gussie Fink-Nottle and Stiffy Byng. Then there is Ian Fleming with Dr. No, Oddjob, and Pussy Galore. There is Joseph Heller with Lieutenant Scheisskopf, Major Major Major, and Milo Minderbinder. There is Terry Southern's unforgettable President Merkin and, of course, Flann O'Brien's Bonaparte O'Coonassa.

Simile and metaphor have always been popular devices for characterization. People have been likened to fish, bugs, mountain crags, cows, bulls, wolves, sheep, horses, sharks, food, mythological gods and goddesses, lions, gazelles, monuments, ideas, ideals, and practically everything else. In *Eugénie Grandet*, Balzac gives us an analogy for old Grandet:

Financially speaking, Monsieur Grandet was a combination of tiger and boa constrictor: he was capable of lying hidden in wait, contemplating his prey for a long time before pouncing. Then, when ready, he would open the jaws of his purse, swallowing a sumptuous meal of golden crowns, and subside quietly once more, like the serpent digesting: impassive, cold, methodical.[15]

It was not Balzac's best moment. The description is graphic, but he had to go far afield—to America and Africa —for his effects (boa constrictors and tigers must play a very small part in the life of small French towns). Furthermore, the "jaws of his purse" are no part of old Grandet himself and Balzac's importation of them is illogical. A metaphor—which is a poetic stretching of logic to begin with—must make as precise and striking a matchup as possible. And, of course, remembering the man who smelled a rat and nipped it in the bud, authors must avoid mixed metaphors.

Simile or metaphor applied to characters should be economical; the taste of the times is against those elaborate, ingenious inventions. Robert Greenwood in his novel *Wagstaff* captures the essence of his central character thus: "Timing his arrival at the station to a minute, Wagstaff bustled through the barrier, looking, in his brightest suit and most hilarious necktie, as joyful as a tree in blossom." And a shy, seventeen-year-old girl in the same book appears and disappears "like a wren in a bramble." Nigel Dennis in *Cards of Identity* (its subject is the problem of identity) notes that Dr. Shubunkin has a face marked "with dozens of seams and grooves. When his eyes flash with analytical interest all the lines become illuminated and run to the center of his face, pointing. It is probable that he got this idea from the electric map system of the Paris Metro." This seems to be reaching a little too hard, but, nevertheless, it is very amusing. The reader should not have to pause to sort out the image, as in the case of Muriel Spark's Louisa Jepp, which is a trifle laborious and complicated. It should be direct and simple and it should not be so striking as to set up an independent existence in the story.

STREAM OF CONSCIOUSNESS

Some critics consider stream of consciousness more a strategy of presenting a character (like capsule characterization or gradual revelation) than a technique for characterization. In *The Novel and the Modern World,* David Daiches says, "Novelists who employ the stream of consciousness would deny that character portrayal is possible for the fiction writer at all: character is a process, not a state, and the truth . . . can be presented only through some attempt to show this process at work." Whatever the terms assigned, however, there can be no denying that stream of consciousness can be useful in revealing a character from the inside.

This is a passage from Barbara Pym's *Excellent Women:*

No sink has ever been built high enough for a reasonably tall person and my back was soon aching with the effort of washing up, especially as yesterday's greasy dishes needed a lot of scrubbing to get them clean. My thoughts went round and round and it occurred to me that if I ever wrote a novel it would be of the "stream of consciousness type" and deal with an hour in the life of a woman at the sink.[16]

We can see how custom and the passage of time have domesticated that once-formidable, avant-garde mystery, the stream of consciousness. Although in undefined form it had been a method for imaginative work as far back as Shakespeare and other Elizabethans, the high fashion it achieved with the publication of Joyce's *Ulysses* and the respectful critical attention afterward accorded even to feeble imitations did a certain amount of harm. Those developments made most beginning writers feel that they must master its tricks or else turn to the advertising business.

There were writers—most now forgotten—who used the method so relentlessly that readers rebelled; and, after World War II, writers also began to rebel. In the 1950s, Angus Wilson said that the reestablishment of a social framework for the novel "has also restored the formal framework of plot, narrative, sub-plot, suspense, or, in some hands, picaresque presentation. . . . If stream of consciousness, interior monologue of the more orthodox kind, cinematic treatments of time and place, and other experimental forms are less used . . . it is because their defects of cumbrousness and monotony have become apparent."

Now that the bloom has rubbed off, stream of consciousness can be seen as a useful device if handled judiciously. It no longer seems necessary to fill page after page with undisciplined thought processes. Thus, a brief history of its use and misuse might be appropriate.

Around 1900, writers with an interest in technique

began to explore the minds of characters in a new way. William James, in *Principles of Psychology*, coined the name "stream of consciousness" to describe it. For the imaginative writer, this became an articulation of the unselective flow of thought and feeling through the mind. Dispensing with "he thought," "he vowed silently," and "he was reminded," the writer could seem to bring the reader into the mind of a character and let him witness half thoughts and impressions that the character himself scarcely realized. And, because we tend to think in phrases and sentence fragments, formal syntax was no longer necessary. Logic, too, had to suffer, except for the wild logic of association that causes one subject to pull another out of the unconscious, and that still another. Present, past, and future are mingled; this place and distant ones rub together; ideas, images, sensations, memories, intuitions flow in the common stream. Molly Bloom's forty-five pages that close *Ulysses* are probably the most famous and most brilliant example.

All this seemed very revolutionary sixty years ago, but today, made commonplace, it can turn up in the narration of romantic novels, novels of suspense, and science fiction. Freud taught us to look inward, and the novelist has tried to bring us into the unguarded center of the self.

The principal method of stream of consciousness is called either interior or internal monologue. The point to stress here is that the monologue has to be controlled by the author. Though the thought-flow is seemingly uncensored, and irrelevance is part of the concept, the author must keep a rein on things and keep moving in one direction, at least. Robert Humphrey (in his *Stream of Consciousness in the Mod-*

ern Novel) makes a useful distinction between direct and indirect interior monologue. The first offers a character's thoughts in full spate with—ostensibly—no author shaping them. Here is a fragment of Molly's reverie on men:

theyre so weak and puling when theyre sick they want a woman to get it well if his nose bleeds youd think it was O tragic and that dyinglooking one off the south circular when he sprained his foot at the choir party at the sugarloaf Mountain the day I wore that dress Miss Stack bringing him flowers the worst old ones she could find at the bottom of the basket anything at all to get into a mans bedroom with her old maids voice trying to imagine he was dying on account of her to never see thy face again though he looked more like a man with his beard grown in the bed father was the same besides I hate bandaging and dosing when he cut his toe with the new razor paring his corns. . . .[17]

It is impossible to excerpt satisfactorily from this famous monologue, but in this passage it is apparent how a vague generalization about the male response to being sick leads Molly to think of specific things: the behavior of Miss Stack, Bloom with a beard, her father paring his corns with a razor. That is the "direction" that Joyce is taking for Molly's thoughts and, of course, it is the main direction. (Reading this today, we can see how dependent even direct interior monologue is on the conventions of written language. Does the unconscious use capitals and connectives? Does the unconscious of uneducated people spell incorrectly? Does the running together of words really convey unconscious thought, or is it a typographical device?)

Indirect interior monologue calls the character by name and uses the third person pronoun "he" or "she," or—far less plausibly—the second person "you." Here the author is more in evidence and the monologue more controlled. Sometimes he even offers commentary or description. There is more coherence in the character's thoughts, not only in syntax but in logic. Humphrey notes that the fundamental quality of the stream is retained because what we see "of consciousness is direct; it is in the idiom and with the peculiarities of the character's psychic processes." As an example, he cites the opening of *Mrs. Dalloway:*

> Mrs. Dalloway said she would buy the flowers herself.
>
> For Lucy had her work cut out for her. The doors would be taken off their hinges; Rumpelmayer's men were coming . . . And then, thought Clarissa Dalloway, what a morning—fresh as if issued to children on a beach.
>
> What a lark! What a plunge! For so it had always seemed to her, when, with a little squeak of the hinges, which she could hear now, she had burst open the French windows and plunged at Bourton into the open air. How fresh, how calm, stiller than this of course, the air was in the early morning; like the flap of a wave; chill and sharp and yet (for a girl of eighteen as she was then) solemn, feeling as she did, standing there at the open window, that something awful was about to happen. . . .[18]

The author directs this passage, yet the language and responses are Clarissa Dalloway's. A certain amount of ellipsis remains—we must guess that Lucy has her work cut out for her because there is going to be a party and that Lucy is a maid. (The caterer's famous name tips us off). When the fresh morning reminds her of childhood days at Bourton, the language changes to that of Clarissa at eighteen: "What a lark! What a plunge!" And so the reader is transported directly into the past by an agile time shift, into a "solemn" morning when "something awful was about to happen" (as it finally will, on this much later day, before the novel ends).

Indirect interior monologue is probably the most generally useful stream-of-consciousness technique. The consciousness is not simply a mind floating somewhere but a consciousness housed in a body, in a real place, probably talking with other people at times. In the next passage, Mrs. Dalloway goes out to buy the flowers and her impressionistic city scenes also tell us that the Dalloways live in Westminster and have been there more than twenty years, that Clarissa has had a serious illness. Big Ben is striking the hour and she is walking down an actual street, surrounded by carriages, motor cars, omnibuses, brass bands, and barrel organs that enter her awareness of "this moment in June." The authorial control of material and skill of organization is evident.

One other stream of consciousness device is that of soliloquy. Humphrey describes this as "the technique of representing the psychic content and processes of a character directly from character to reader without the presence of an author, but with the audience tacitly assumed." This is a rather formidable definition, but a simple example may make it clear. A salesman who has just failed to close an important business deal returns to his motel room and there, in solitude, begins to rehash the events of the interview and to build up a defense for the way he has handled things. The imaginary "audience" would be his employer, to whom he would have to give an account the next day.

A more sophisticated example is Eudora Welty's story "Why I Live at the P. O." It is the relentless monologue of the China Grove, Mississippi, postmistress, "Sister," who has lately quarreled with her family and moved into the post office. This is a story about a serious personality disturbance but written with such gaiety that the grim subject momentarily becomes a comedy. It begins:

> I was getting along fine with Mama, Papa-Daddy and Uncle Rondo until my sister Stella-Rondo just separated from her husband and came back home again. Mr. Whitaker! Of course I went with Mr. Whitaker first, when he first appeared here in China Grove taking "Pose Yourself" photos, and Stella-Rondo broke us up. Told him I was one-sided. Bigger on one side than the other, which is a deliberate, calculated falsehood. . . .[19]

Sister, in imagination, is trying to justify herself to the collective world of China Grove. Every wounding remark made by her family is remembered verbatim; her own retorts are cherished for their triumphant accuracy. " 'Very well,' I says. 'But I take the fern. Even you, Mama, can't stand there and deny that I'm the one that watered that fern.' "

Any stream-of-consciousness technique requires caution in its use. It can be as boring as the nonstop talker in the plane seat beside you. It sacrifices narrative movement to the circuitous, associative demands of the unconscious. And, of course, it may demand that the reader enter into the consciousness of a character he dislikes. These are the risks—

and the writer should weigh them before he decides to use one.

Fiction writers, beginning with the first great anthology, *The Ocean of Story*, have always been fond of dreams. The Freudian age has made them even fonder. The ancient story-tellers usually wanted to produce some prophecy or omen by means of a dream, and the moderns usually want to give some insight into a character's unconscious. In the majority of cases, the psychological use of the device turns out to be quite as boring as the prophetic. A writer should always ask himself, "Is there any other way I can do this without putting my character to sleep?" If so, he should avoid the dream—and especially avoid it at the beginning of a novel, where it is likely to have a soporific effect on the reader before the first few pages are turned.

CHARACTER TODAY

Although Mary McCarthy's forebodings about the disappearance of character in fiction did not prove to be very prophetic, there is, nevertheless, something of the kind among the fashionable minimalist writers of the mid-1980s. To quote again from Madison Bell's *Harper's* article "Less Is Less," their fiction "ignores or eliminates distinctions among the people it renders." Characters are "as facelessly uniform as the people on television"; or they "resemble rats negotiating a maze that the reader can see and they cannot"; or they are "neutral inhabitants of neutral environments [the condominium and the mall]" and they "act without intention . . . or will." (Mr. Bell mistakenly blames this trend on book publishers and their eagerness to sell books.)

There is nothing to prove—and much to disprove—that Raymond Carver or Ann Beattie is uninterested in character. The minimal style, however, does tend to pare everything down to a few strokes and most of the traditional elements of fiction—dramatic scene, setting, a sense of the past, and so on—are ruthlessly cut. The stories are supposed to be as stark as a four-line sketch by Picasso—and thus as striking. Sometimes they work, as the best of Amy Hempel's stories in *Reasons to Live* work, just because the minimal lines are taut and exact.

Notes to Chapter 4

1. New York: Modern Library, 1938; p. 87.
2. Garden City, N.Y.: Doubleday & Co., 1983; p. 11.
3. New York: Signet, 1962; p. 28.
4. Salem, New Hampshire: Ayer Co., 1977; p. 34.
5. New York: Walter J. Black, 1947; pp. 37, 62.
6. Philadelphia: J. B. Lippincott Co., 1957; pp. 9, 13.
7. From *The Stories of John Cheever* (New York: Alfred A. Knopf, 1978), p. 161.
8. New York: Charles Scribner's Sons, 1952; pp. 12–13.
9. Boston: Houghton Mifflin Co., 1982; p. 45.
10. New York: Viking Press, 1952; pp. 79, 81.
11. Garden City, N.Y.: Doubleday & Co., 1938; pp. 15–16.

12. From *The World of Aldous Huxley* (New York: Harper & Row, 1947), pp. 343–44.

13. New York: New American Library, 1964; p. 167.

14. From H. T. Lowe-Porter, trans. *Stories of Three Decades* (New York: Alfred A. Knopf, 1936), p. 404.

15. Henry Reed, trans. (New York: New American Library 1964), p. 20.

16. New York: E. P. Dutton, 1952; p. 19.

17. New York: Random House, 1934; p. 723.

18. New York: Harcourt, Brace & Co., 1925; pp. 3–5.

19. From *The Selected Stories of Eudora Welty* (New York: Modern Library, 1954), p. 89.

FIVE

POINT OF VIEW

ANGLES OF VISION

The time is the ninth century. The place is a lonely road in the mountains near Kyoto. A nobleman and his bride are riding along and they are joined by another traveler, who lures them into a cedar grove nearby. There, the traveler— a robber—overpowers and binds the nobleman and rapes his wife. Then the robber, moved by the wife's plea, unties the nobleman and duels with him until he kills him—according to the robber's later account. No, according to the wife. She says that the robber fled after the rape and that her husband, filled with shame, begged her to kill him. She did the deed, intending to kill herself as well but failing. Not so, according to the nobleman who (speaking through a medium) says that he finally killed himself. Again, not so says a woodcutter who witnessed the episode and gives a fourth version.

The story of *Rashomon* is probably the most famous modern lesson in point of view, thanks to a powerful movie made by Akira Kurosawa. The movie is based on a short story titled "In a Grove" by the talented Japanese writer Ryuno-suke Akutagawa. And it is no coincidence that the idea of conflicting viewpoints on the same event is to be found in Robert Browning's verse novel *The Ring and the Book*, because Akutagawa was a student of Victorian English literature.

The subject of *Rashomon* is, of course, jesting Pilate's question "What is truth?" But the fictional-technique question is "How do different viewers perceive or misperceive what happened?" In most cases, we would expect every point of view to be falsified by self-interest. Each of the three people in that blood-spattered grove should be ready to blame the crime on another. But it does not happen that way. Each confesses to be the killer, which suggests that all are sincerely trying to tell the truth.

Akutagawa's tale ends with the question that faces most authors at the beginning: through whose eyes should we see? The question did not seem to bother earlier generations of novelists; Moll Flanders was, for Defoe, the only person qualified to describe her own life. To the eighteenth-century French novelist Choderlos de Laclos, it seemed natural to write his *Dangerous Acquaintances*, a complicated intrigue, from the different viewpoints of fourteen characters. But, with the beginning of the modern novel, specifically with Henry James, the choice of a vision or visions became troublesome. James always sought for the right personality or "central intelligence" through which to tell his story, and in the prefaces to his novels (collected in *The Art of Fiction*), he discusses his theory—which has had considerable influence on the novelists who followed him.

Because point of view is a matter of the personal, or impersonal, angles from which a story is apprehended, one convenient way to talk about it is by means of a diagram. The reader is warned that the diagram is no more than a drawing of the possibilities, an abstraction from real fiction.

THE DIAGRAM

The Gamma family is enjoying a picnic in a clearing in the woods. There are three of them, father, mother, and a son of ten years. They think they are all alone, but it so happens that a neighbor of theirs, Mr. Beta, is standing a little way off, hidden by some trees. He can see them and overhear what they are saying. Neither the Gammas nor Beta, however, realize that there is still a fifth personality present—a certain mysterious and powerful being known as Alpha. He stands some distance away, at the top of a small hill, and he can view the other people and all the woods around them without being seen himself.

In the course of the picnic, there is only one happening that concerns us. Mrs. Gamma and her husband disagree over something. The disagreement flares up into a quarrel and he angrily slaps her across the face. That is all to the incident, but there is still a story to be told.

POSSIBLE POINTS OF VIEW:
THE GAMMAS

Around the picnic cloth there are, obviously, three points of view, three different pairs of eyes and three different minds behind them. The author has to make his crucial choice among them because these are not simply three different registers of the same event; each one is potentially an entirely different story. That is, the facts in the life of the Gamma family might remain (unlike in *Rashomon*) a matter of common agreement, but the point of view is the first means by which those facts pass into fiction, into an artful treatment of the facts. As in Henry James's debates with himself, it becomes a question of whose story.

Assume that the author chooses Mrs. Gamma's point of view, and assume a few more things about her. She bitterly resents the slap because the sting is mental more than physical. She has tried to be a good wife and mother, but in recent years Gamma has begun to mistreat her. She remembers the promising career she gave up to marry him; she remembers the richer and more considerate man she rejected in favor of Gamma. This version of the story is going to be told by an unappreciated, wronged, and injured person.

Now assume that the author changes his mind—perhaps Mrs. Gamma strikes him as being too full of self-pity and therefore boring. He next considers Mr. Gamma, a tough-minded, self-centered man whose main interest in life is his business. Long ago he shed the brief sentimentality of early marriage, and now he looks at his wife and son as things that have happened to him and that he must bear with. Though he does not know the term, he views his wife as a kind of injustice collector because she seems to create small crises that result in hurting herself. He thinks of himself as a very patient man, but this time she has gone a little too far, and he slaps her. It isn't really to hurt her but to shut her up and stop that constant sarcasm and complaint.

But the author rejects Gamma as well. It may be that his hard ego is too difficult to work with or that his intelligence is too coarse for the theme the story will have. A point of view must be flexible and subtle enough so that the author can explore many possibilities of his story. This brings him to the boy.

A child's point of view has the charm of innocence and the fresh virtue of honesty. It offers an immediate contrast between the venal, scheming adults and the young girl or boy who watches them and wonders. Further, there is a belief common to authors (but not necessarily to mothers) that children are inordinately perceptive. As Henry James said about his child-observer in his preface to *What Maisie Knew*, "I should have to invest her with perceptions easily and almost infinitely quickened." The result has been a tradition of exceptionally successful novels through young eyes—beginning with the young Jane Eyre, David, Pip, Maisie, and Jim Hawkins to modern examples in the novels of Marilynne Robinson *(Housekeeping),* Anne Bernays *(Growing Up Rich)* and Paul Theroux *(The Mosquito Coast).*

Suppose, however, that our writer decided against Gamma junior. He reasoned that the child's (or adolescent's) point of view has grown nearly into a situational cliché in modern fiction simply because so many writers have used it. The charm of limited knowledge, unusual sensitivity, and perfect candor has been dulled by the boredom that comes from overuse of a good thing.

Thus the author turns again, this time to the somewhat removed observer, Mr. Beta. He is, of course that device of fiction known as the narrator, or the "dramatized narrator," to be more exact.

THE NARRATOR

Beta lives in the same world as the Gamma family. If he wanted to, he could step into the picnic glade and speak to them. In some fiction, he will play a role in the story to come, but it will be a secondary role; in some stories, his role will be even less than secondary. The author has created him to act as his agent and reporter. His assignment is to survey the whole scope of the story and to recount it with a breadth of knowledge and a relative objectivity that none of the direct participants could possess. He cannot give us the sudden frightened sensation of a child who sees his father hit his mother. On the other hand, he has the advantage of being able to see the faces of all three actors in the glade and to use his insight about what emotions they are experiencing.

"I am not I; thou art not he or she; they are not they," reads a disclaimer prefacing *Brideshead Revisited.* The skillful fiction writer wants to emphasize "I am not I" and to draw a distinction between his own deliberately concealed personality and that of his narrator. The narrator observes selectively, but, more important, he is an interpreter in his own individual way. *The Great Gatsby* is not just anybody's story; it is the story of Jay Gatsby as only Nick Carraway (as distinct from Fitzgerald) could tell it. Only "Bub" (we never learn his real name) could relate Raymond Carver's notable story "Cathedral"; James Dickey's *Deliverance* would be quite a different (and lesser) novel if told by anyone other than Edward

Gentry (who, however, is a leading character rather than a detached narrator).

The agent device came from the earliest days of fiction, but it was adopted and made more sophisticated by the James-Conrad-Ford generation of writers. Conrad invented Marlow to act as his voice, and Marlow grew so idiosyncratic that James called him "that preposterous master mariner." Ford invented a plain, simple American from Philadelphia, only to find that underneath was a strange and complicated psychology. James invented a nice, conventional governess to tell his ghost story, and slowly she revealed herself as a fantasist and neurotic. The narrator-agent has a habit of defying the author's plans and taking on a definite personality of his own. And, in the best fiction, so he should.

The modern employment of this kind of narrator came from a revulsion against the habit eighteenth- and nineteenth-century writers had of interrupting. It is called an "authorial intrusion," and it occurs when the author in his own person drops in for a chat with the reader. Thackeray puts aside his "puppet theater" for a time in order to talk to us; Trollope tells us what is going to happen later on; Fielding tells us jokes. It was a most awkward invasion of the story's privacy. Worse, it destroyed any sense of real experience that the story may have built up.

Thus, the narrator as agent was called upon to carry out a special mission. He became the author's point of view transformed (in small ways or large), personified, and humanized. That gives him the ability to generalize as alter ego for the author and to comment on events and characters as no one else can. Along with that, he usually has the advantage of emotional detachment from the story and—unlike the main participants—a chance to gather information from many sources.

But he is always an agent; he accepts a lot of limitations. He cannot be omniscient, as the author is. He can guess shrewdly what is going on in the minds of the principal actors, but he cannot enter into those minds. With the delicate instrument of interior exploration denied, he has to rely on the cruder tools of attempted mind reading or insight, on what he hears and observes, on hearsay that comes his way.

There are still other areas that the rules of plausibility deny him, and sometimes authors forget and invade those forbidden places. Ishmael is the narrator of *Moby-Dick*, but now and then Melville overrides him and lets us hear things that Ishmael is not privileged to hear. Nelly Dean is sometimes the narrator of *Wuthering Heights*, and she includes in her account exact transcripts of letters she could not have seen unless she was in the habit of reading her master's mail —but we are never told that was the case. Dowell, Ford Madox Ford's odd narrator in *The Good Soldier*, describes in detail scenes that took place in a remote country he has never visited—and with no apparent source of this knowledge. In short, the author who hires a narrator as his point of view has to accept that the narrator is human. The author cannot transfer any of his godlike, demiurgical privileges.

A more subtle limitation he has to accept is his agent's individuality. At his best, the narrator has a voice of his own, a definite outlook on the world, and he thus gives the fiction a "character." To put it another way, the fiction becomes cohesive and firm because there is someone tangible in command. But, to make this work, the narrator has to possess a personality that is well knit, relatively simple—and honest.

Strange complications appear when it is otherwise. Conrad's Marlow relates *Youth: A Narrative* sometimes as a verbose old salt, sometimes as a pompous homespun philosopher, and sometimes as a breezy tale-teller. The effect on the story is not good. Again, another narrator might be miscast, hampering and distorting the story rather than directing its flow.

There is an even more dangerous and interesting potential in the character of the narrator, and that is the element of ambiguity. When the leading woman character or the leading male character tells the story, we know what her or his biases are. When the personally involved narrator is telling it, we know how he is likely to qualify the truth. Mrs. Gamma says there is no reason in the world why her husband must spend almost every evening away from home. But we have heard her nag—and we can guess why he does.

This clear author-reader understanding gets more obscure when there is a Mr. Beta recounting his version of the story. The basic question becomes one of trying to measure him. We do not imagine that he will lie to us deliberately, but we have never seen him in context, we have never watched him as part of the drama, and so we find it hard to judge his version of the truth. (*The Rhetoric of Fiction* by Wayne Booth is one of the best commentaries on this subject, with its excellent analysis of "reliable" and "unreliable" types of narrators.)

One of the most famous debates in modern literary criticism was over the version of the story given by the governess who relates Henry James's *The Turn of the Screw*. She is the narrator but is also, at times, a chief participant. The "true" meaning of her words and actions has been interpreted in different ways by different critics, but none has been clearly convincing. Booth remarks that "few of us feel happy with a situation in which we cannot decide whether the subject is two evil children as seen by a naive but well-meaning governess or two innocent children as seen by a hysterical, destructive governess." He adds that when James created a "seriously-flawed narrator," he was no longer able to mediate between the peculiarities of his teller and the peculiarities of the drama. That is, the unknown in the woman becomes the unknown of the story—and that is almost more ambiguity than any story can bear.

I, SHE, OR HE—EVEN WE OR YOU

Actor or narrator point of view—either can come to us in the first-person singular or third-person singular. The choice depends on how much intimacy and how much identification the writer wants to establish between reader and teller. Each choice has it merits and its risks.

Henry James called the first-person singular "that accurst autobiographic form which puts a premium on the loose, the improvised, the cheap and the easy." He thought that it destroyed the necessary detachment between the writer and his subject. Like many other overstatements about technique, this has its solid grain of truth.

The first and simplest fallacy about it is that tendency for naive writer and reader to assume that there must be a one-to-one correspondence between the author and the "I" of the story. This often leads the writer to limit matters to bald reality. When the critic suggests certain imaginative improvements, the writer is likely to reply, "No, she has to be the way I've described her because that's the way she was," or "I couldn't say that—it didn't happen that way." This kind of lock on the imagination is most frequent in a first-person narrative.

The form also carries a great temptation for self-indulgence, that is, the loose, cheap, and easy habit of displaying oneself rather than the story. This kind of ego-trip results in some garrulous, arch, and irrelevant first-person narrators in fiction. A story should not be confused with a screen test, a psychiatrist's couch, an advertisement for oneself, or an *apologia pro vita mea.*

Still, there are many novels and stories that have a genuine need for a first-person teller, provided that the "I" is created an independent being. The autobiographic form can establish an intimacy and involvement for the reader in a way that the third person cannot. It is easy to identify with "I" in a story, while it takes longer to trust those strangers known as "he" or "she." There are good and calculated reasons why the first person tells such diverse tales as Hemingway's *Farewell to Arms,* Robert Graves's *I, Claudius,* Saul Bellow's *Humboldt's Gift,* William Trevor's *Fools of Fortune,* or Margaret Atwood's *The Handmaid's Tale;* all somewhat different reasons but all basically alike. The first-person voice gives an impression of being direct, candid, and trustworthy. We assume at once that it is the voice of a good person—until, in some novels, we find that isn't true.

The agreeable quality about this kind of narration is that
it gives the sense of listening to a real human tell us his or
her personal story. We assume that the "I," having gone
through certain experiences, now can look back at them with
wisdom and maturity. The reader suspects that the experiences somehow changed that life for better or for worse, and
that the "I" who tells the story is a changed person from the
younger "I" to whom it all happened. There is a special,
living quality about this because we all look back at our
histories and our former selves in the same way. "He was
. . . she was," on the other hand, begins a story about strangers inhabiting one definite time in the past.

Using the third person does not automatically do away
with the accurst autobiographic failings—take Hemingway's
Across the River and into the Trees or any of Thomas Wolfe's
novels, for example—but it helps. One of its advantages is a
certain psychological freedom it gives an author. It is easier
to make "he" or "she" do or experience things that never
happened in the real life of the writer. It is psychologically
difficult to make "I" ridiculous, boastful, sordid, dishonest,
stupid, or hard-hearted (even though some authors have done
it unintentionally). "Being talented and clever, I soon rose to
the top on Wall Street." "My main problem now was how to
chop up her corpse and dispose of it." Readers lose heart very
soon after such announcements. That is the reason why so
many of the "I's" of fiction are modest, reasonable, and
rather colorless.

In André Malraux's great novel *Man's Fate*, there is a
scene in which a young man called Kyo listens to his own
voice on some records the revolutionists are using to send

secret messages. He does not recognize his own voice. And so it is that there are very common things about ourselves of which we are not aware. It is easier for the author to show such traits about the third person as point of view than about the first person.

There are still two other persons, less manageable and less frequently met, and they are "we" and "you."

"We" is taken as the viewpoint in one of Donald Barthelme's satiric, surrealist stories titled "The Educational Experience," where it seems to represent the faculty taking students through an exhibition of the university curriculum. A much more ambitious use of it appears in Joan Chase's novel, *During the Reign of the Queen of Persia.* There the "we" stands for the collective point of view of two sets of teenage sisters, so closely identified with one another by age, feelings, and blood ties that they can speak as one: "Sometimes we thought we were the same—same blood, same rights of inheritance." Luckily, the novel is a short one, because this agreeable tour de force is also limiting.

Another tour de force is the occasional choice of the second-person singular as the point of view. In Jay McInerney's well-received novel *Bright Lights, Big City*—a fast excursion through the labyrinth of Manhattan life—"you" becomes both the hero and the viewpoint: "You are not the kind of guy who would be at a place like this at this time of the morning. But here you are, and you cannot say that the terrain is entirely unfamiliar, although the details are fuzzy. You are at a nightclub talking with a girl with a shaved head." What seems like no more than a clever contrivance at first later becomes a natural part of this lively novel.

First-person plural and second-person singular are interesting enough as occasional novelties, but they tend to become tiresome over any long stretch or if encountered very often. Because one is a collective persona and the other a form of address that tends to be as impersonal as a "Hey, you!" the reader finds that there is really no protagonist or any individual point of view.

THE ALL-KNOWING MR. ALPHA

As the actual author and the real teller of the fiction, Alpha is omnipotent, omniscient, and omnipresent. Assume that he has discarded all other possible narrators and accepted the responsibility himself—he is still faced with the necessity of making the story seem a natural sequence of happenings, not his arbitrary construction. There will be times when he will wish to borrow the vision of a character and see things from that person's point of view for a while. But there will be other times when the author is entirely responsible, commenting, abridging, or taking a panoramic glance. At such times, he is the only possible narrator, and his obligation is to do his work plausibly, quietly, and without proclaiming himself. Critics have spoken of the "invisible narrator," which is a somewhat misleading term. A voice is a very real presence in fiction, and the sophisticated reader is usually aware of that voice's identity. The author's tone should be consonant with the fictional surroundings, tuned, as it were, to the pitch of the story. It should not be the voice of a drill sergeant ordering his characters around, or a loud whisper giving cues from the prompter's box, or the voice of a lecturer who has stopped the show to fill us in with the background information.

Even though there are many risks, Alpha's direct command of the story is, finally, the most versatile, flexible, and privileged of all the methods. The variety of tactics open to him include these:

1. He can borrow and use any one of several points of view as it suits his purpose.
2. He can offer us the theater of "showing, not telling" objectivity as he wishes.
3. He can analyze his own story through comment (as long as he does this subtly enough).
4. He can take a panoramic view, describing events that happen simultaneously or scenes that are widely separated in geography—things that a character narrator could not possibly cover completely.
5. He can discover multiple traits of the characters plausibly enough without having to look for them through another's limited point of view.

Writing smooth transitions is all-important here because the metamorphosis of Alpha as he takes on the eyes and mask of Mrs. Gamma, moves to an impersonal viewing of a scene, then assumes the persona of the young Gamma, and finally reverts to the all-seeing vision of Alpha must never strike the reader as a mere magical trick. The writer often runs into trouble when he tries to do too many changes too quickly.

There is, for instance, the kind of scene during which the writer wants to dip into the thoughts or feelings of different characters for just a moment. The purpose is a survey of contrasts:

> The fire began to spread and now nearly the whole wing of the old resort hotel was obscured by smoke. Fletcher thought of the pile of banknotes in the steel box and he could almost see them turning brown at the edges and crisping like dead leaves. His wife, standing next to him with a stained and troubled face, thought only of the dead child's sweater she had carried with her all these twelve years. She shivered at the thought of the flames licking at it. Joan Parsons was reflecting, "Now he'll never be able to drag me to this boring place again," while Dick Parsons was thinking, "I wonder if the insurance on our clothes and luggage would be enough to pay for a divorce." The fire began to sweep in gusts along the clapboards and one of the firemen yelled for them to stand back.

This has a nervous and artificial effect because too much is crammed together and the leapfrogging of different points of view is too obvious. In this case, it would be better to remain with one point of view and produce some of the reactions in the form of dialogue and reserve some of them for later.

There is a scene in *War and Peace* that shows Tolstoy, perhaps the preeminent novelist of the nineteenth century, as sometimes guilty of this kind of indeterminate shifting. It takes place just after the battle of Borodino and the Russian army is in retreat. Kutuzov, the commander, has called his generals together in a peasant's cottage for a council. Tolstoy's main purpose was to stage a debate between Kutuzov and General Bennigsen and to show how Kutuzov decided to

abandon Moscow to the French. But he also had an inspiration for getting an odd and interesting angle on the scene.
Why not show it from the point of view of a little peasant girl
who watches history in the making as she sits behind a stove?
But the interesting notion and the necessary idea do not work
together. Here are some samples that show the mixture (the
name indicates whose point of view is being used at the
moment).

> The adjutant Kaisarov: he would have drawn back a curtain
> from the window facing Kutuzov, but the latter shook his head
> angrily at him and Kaisarov saw saw that his highness did not care
> for them to see his face.
> The author: Round the peasant's deal table, on which lay maps,
> plans, pencils and papers, there was such a crowd that the orderlies
> brought in another bench and set it near the table.
> The little girl, Malasha: she saw the council in quite a different
> light. It seemed to her that the whole point at issue was a personal
> struggle between "Grandad" and "Longcoat," as she called Ben-
> nigsen . . . she noted with glee that "Grandad's" words had put
> "Longcoat" down.
> The author: The words that had thus affected Bennigsen were
> Kutuzov's quietly and softly uttered comment.[1]

It must have become evident to Tolstoy quite early that
the little girl could comprehend no more than the fact that two
men, one sympathetic-seeming and one not, were quarreling.
The real business of the episode is presented objectively,
which accomplishes its business, and the nice idea of having
a peasant child register an important moment in Russian

history appeared, on second thought, to be unworkable, and so the little girl remains simply to confuse the scene.

The moral is that even the greatest author has to be wary of getting himself into such a technical jam. He should don an individual point of view only when his reasons are clear. The reason for preempting a special point of view is to scrutinize the scene more strikingly than the objective viewpoint could—and yet just as clearly.

It is always a good idea—as noted before—to choose one point of view and to stick with it throughout the scene or episode. That is the only way to preserve a contrast, say, between the point of view and the tenor of the scene. An idealistic young campaign worker witnesses a conversation among some corrupt old political henchmen. Maintaining her viewpoint is essential. In some other context, the dynamic between point of view and scene could be one of enthusiastic agreement, suspicion, edification, or whatever.

After the scene, the author is free to shift to another point of view. Percy Lubbock explains it this way: He says that the character who has taken on the viewpoint and has become an "open consciousness," now becomes "sealed" again. He or she drops back into the plane of ordinary people observed from the outside. "He may mingle with the rest, engage in talk with them, and his presence and his talk are no more to the fore than theirs."

The reason for assuming one character's point of view should be purposeful because here is a good opportunity for a double judgment. The author makes certain assessments of the scene through his character's feelings or biases and he also makes a judgment on the character. Say, for instance, that Tolstoy had chosen to view his post-Borodino council through the eyes of a brilliant general who had actually been the one to save the day at Borodino—and who was listening with contempt to the pair of bunglers, Kutuzov and Bennigsen. That would give both the scene and the observer very interesting functions that they do not now have—the quick perceptions of the line officer who has been in the thick of battle as compared with the slow thinking of the old headquarters generals who are just beginning to grasp the situation. (This was indeed the historical case. The much-underrated Russian general was Barclay de Tolly, and the claims for him are laid out in a brilliant biography, *The Commander*, by Michael and Diana Josselson.)

Or, on the other hand, Tolstoy might have created a powerful scene if he had written it in the impersonal, dramatic mode. We could watch the formidable Bennigsen sticking to his sentimental dogma ("The holy and ancient capital of Russia" must be defended), Kutuzov's eloquent argument to the contrary, and finally the emerging realization that the debate itself is meaningless and that the loss of the city is a foregone conclusion.

With the pure use of a single point of view, the writer can theorize or judge without difficulty ("I realized now what a hypocrite she was," or "He felt grateful to find at least one act of kindness in this desolate city") as long as he stays within the subjective limitation. When he has established the detached point of view and wishes to generalize, he must make the reader deduce for himself (we, the readers, have seen her behavior and we conclude that she is a hypocrite).

Either method works well enough in the short story, but

the novelist has to be careful. The best novelists always have two sides to their natures—the recording, descriptive, story-telling side; and the meaningful, critical, judgmental side. Modern novelists—probably in reaction against their moralizing literary ancestors—have felt uneasy about moral weighing and measuring and have tended to rely much on the "showing, not telling" procedures. Most novelists write either out of a sense of justice or a sense of injustice, but they are reluctant to preach sermons. The art of the modern novel, therefore is marked by what is implied, what left out, and what is said through symbols—the covert language of fiction in the twentieth century.

There is no rule or formula to tell the writer when he should try overt interpretation or generalization. In practice, it is generally a place in the story where no implication or indirection will carry the message. Comment of this kind should have a precise relationship to the material of the story, should be lucid, firm, and economical in its style. Joseph Conrad was a writer who liked to speak out about the general —or philosophical—concerns in his fiction. Here is an example from his *The Nigger of the Narcissus:*

James Wait rallied again. He lifted his head and turned bravely at Donkin, who saw a strange face, an unknown face, a fantastic and grimacing mask of despair and fury. Its lips moved rapidly; and hollow, moaning, whistling sounds filled the cabin with a vague mutter full of menace, complaint and desolation, like a far-off murmur of a rising wind. Wait shook his head; rolled his eyes; he denied, cursed, threatened—and not a word had the strength to pass beyond the sorrowful pout of those black lips. It was incomprehensible and disturbing; a gibberish of emotions, a frantic dumb-show of speech pleading for impossible things, promising a shadowy vengeance.[2]

Conrad's description of the dying black sailor is thoroughly charged with the author's commentary. Only the author is capable of reading all that meaning—and it is a valuable meaning for the story—into the agonized expression of James Wait. There is simply no other way to do it without obvious fakery and the small scene succeeds just because Conrad takes it in his own hands.

On the other hand, when Conrad sets all sails for a philosophical passage, he can be as prolix and windy as any nineteenth-century novelist. For example, another passage from the same story goes, "On men reprieved by its disdainful mercy, the immortal sea confers in its justice the full privilege of desired unrest. Through the perfect wisdom of its grace they are not permitted to meditate at ease upon the complicated and acrid savour of existence . . ." and so on. A splendid novelist and a master of indirect meaning (e.g., "The Secret Sharer" and *Heart of Darkness*), Conrad was also at times an unlicensed philosopher who did not know when to let well enough alone.

A recent example of a novelist viewing and speaking above the head of his character comes from Leslie Epstein's remarkable Holocaust novel, *The King of the Jews*. I. C. Trumpelman, the Jewish Elder who has become the Nazi puppet ruler of the ghetto, goes to the municipal baths and has a hallucinatory experience. He finds the baths crowded with the local Nazi officials, the steam nearly overcomes him, and he has a vision of a world pogrom. At last he faints and this is the state of things when he comes to:

> The Jews are a desert people. Dry. Arid. Always moving around. Not like the Others, a forest folk, deeply rooted, used to mists and dampness and fogs. Thus there was a possibility Trumpelman had only fainted; perhaps he had had too much steam. Indeed, he did awake somewhat later. He opened both his eyes. Everything was quiet and shadowy and still. The fire in the fire pit had gone out. There was no one in the upper benches. No one in the benches below. The municipal bath was deserted. Had anyone ever been there?
>
> But when the Elder attempted to rise, he could not. He wanted to lift his head; his head would not move. He saw out the open top of the dome. The sky, not really dark, was covered with a powdery light, as if on its surface one professor had just erased all of another's equations.[3]

The authorial voice has multiple resources. It can take panoramic views—for instance, E. M. Forster's trashy town of Chandrapore strewn along its river, as cited in chapter 2. It can shift scene as need be to another location. It can report serially on events that actually take place at the same time. It can observe abstractly or poetically in language that would be beyond the reach of the character—as Epstein does with that evocative image about the sky.

Perhaps Alpha's greatest gift is to deal with character in more various descriptive and developmental ways than can any limited point of view—or collection of viewpoints. Conrad divines the depths of James Wait's despair in words—

Wait's shipmates can feel it but they do not have the power to express it. Wait cannot articulate it himself. The detached, scenic view could show no more than his tortured face, as in a silent movie. James Wait becomes human solely because Conrad is there to speak for him and over him. Trumpelman, who might have been seen as a despicable petty tyrant, becomes a figure of tragedy because Epstein can envision the tale as a tragedy and can be its voice.

Finally, there is no formula that gives an answer to the question "Through whose eyes should we see?" The answer depends on the nature of the story and the angle or angles from which the author chooses to watch it. If one viewpoint proves too narrow, the writer should reassess it and then try another or a combination of others. There is a good reason why most men writers adopt a masculine viewpoint and most woman writers a woman's—it takes great skill to imagine the world through a different biology and psychology. Yet remember Emma Bovary, Anna Karenina, Molly Bloom, and other women of men's creation. Remember Heathcliff, Archbishop Jean Latour, Richard Mahony, Major Yeates, R. M., and Sam Pollit, who were so expertly personified by women writers. There is no reason why an author should not dare cross the line of gender to find his or her point of view.

There has been, in recent years, a similar feeling of taboo against crossing racial or cultural lines in search of a viewpoint. Some black writers have declared that no white person could possibly understand a black sensibility well enough to write from its perspective. If that is true, the opposite must be true as well—and black writers must forever be confined to purely black experience. All of which would lead to a literary segregation of Jews from Gentiles, Asians from Europeans, or straights from gays, perhaps. The only sensible guide, of course, is the writer's true estimate of his own powers of metamorphosis. It remains as a wonderful challenge seldom taken up. In English literature, one major success is *A Passage to India.*

Whose story? The answer is so important because it begins the whole sequence of a fiction much like the sequence of the House that Jack Built. There has to be a Jack to build the house before we can have a cat that ate the mouse, before we can have a dog that chased the cat, and so on.

Notes to Chapter 5

1. Constance Garnett, trans. (New York: Modern Library, 1931), p. 781.
2. From *The Portable Conrad* (New York: Viking Press, 1957), p. 432.
3. New York: Coward, McCann & Geoghegan, 1979; p. 273.

SIX

BACKGROUND; SETTING; PLACE; MILIEU

"THE CROSSROADS OF CIRCUMSTANCE"

John Gardner believed that you could judge an author's talent by the "relative accuracy and originality of his 'eye.' " In his *On Becoming a Novelist,* he said that experienced writers know that "careless seeing can undermine a project. Imagining the fictional scene imprecisely . . . the writer may be tricked into developing his situation in some way that is unconvincing." Most good fiction writers and practically all great writers have had a visual imagination. (There are a few exceptions. James Joyce, for instance, had a weak visual imagination but a powerful aural recollection and imagination that made up for it.) The visual writer can read faces, interpret rooms and their furnishings, scrutinize houses and architecture, quarters of towns, vistas of landscapes, sea and coastline, and the weather that mingles with place. He takes enjoyment in the sheer configuration and color of the world.

We find as examples some well-known novels in which

surroundings shape both the people and events. Could the story of *Wuthering Heights* have taken place in London? Suppose Henry James had tried to set *Washington Square* in Detroit? Try to imagine William Faulkner's Yoknapatawpha County in the middle of Nebraska.

There is no moving them. That savage wind off the moors, the stone-colored sky, and the grim houses remote from one another make a world of their own. Of course Emily Brontë's Yorkshire is as much fiction as it is fact, the beauty and violence as much in her mind as in the landscape. As always with place-imbued writers, she has transformed recognizable geography into a consistent vision, the only setting where her particular story could be played out.

During the years that Yoknapatawpha County was created and populated, Adolf Hitler was on his way to power in Germany; weekly, 115 million people went to the movies in the United States and learned new ways of talking, dressing, and behaving; an economic depression gripped the world; the Spanish Civil War broke out; England went through a crisis when Edward VIII had to abdicate; World War II loomed on the horizon. All this time, Faulkner's county had its own history, its own great events, passions, disasters, quite apart from the rest of the world and untouched by it.

We come now to those writers who seem either to lack a visual place sense or to employ it sparingly. Often, like Joyce, they have an acute sense of hearing, especially for speech—and how much of their worlds is built of sounds! J. D. Salinger's is an almost-bare stage set, with an occasional signboard to tell us the locale: "We got to the Edmont Hotel," Holden Caulfield reports, "and I checked in. . . . They gave

me this very crumby room, with nothing to look out of the
window at except the other side of the hotel. . . . I thought
I'd go downstairs and see what the hell was going on in the
Lavender Room. . . . It wasn't very crowded, but they gave
me a lousy table, anyway—way in the back. . . . The band
was putrid." Later: "I sat down in this vomity-looking chair
in the lobby. . . . The whole lobby . . . smelled like fifty million
dead cigars." (From *The Catcher in the Rye.*) Several chapters
are set in the Edmont Hotel, but all we know of it is that it
is on Manhattan's West Side and that Holden finds it disgust-
ing in a general way. This minimal background is sufficient
for Salinger's purposes, and the setting could be almost any
third-rate hotel in America.

Somerset Maugham's fictional eyesight was a little better, but not much: "He led me up a noble flight of heavily
carpeted stairs . . . we entered the strangers' dining room and
we were its only occupants. It was a room of some size, very
clean and white, with an Adam window." (From *Cakes and
Ale.*) Ada Leverson's charm has far more to do with her
dialogue than with her settings. Here is an example of her
summary kind of description: "They were sitting in a dismal
little drawing room in one of the smallest houses in a dreary
street in Belgravia. The room was crowded with dateless,
unmeaning furniture, and disfigured by muddled, mistaken
decorations." (From *Love's Shadow.*) These are not direct
visual impressions of the place but, seemingly, details remarked on later. "My dear, did you notice how muddled and
mistaken those decorations were?" and "She does live in a
dreary little street, doesn't she?"

The happiest gift for a writer is the ability to hear the

individual voice and to see the ground on which the character stands simultaneously. Scott Fitzgerald promises this when he has Nick Carraway say: "It was a matter of chance that I should have rented a house in one of the strangest communities in North America. It was on that slender, riotous island which extends itself due east of New York. . . ." All at once, we get the sense of a personality interacting with a setting— and "riotous" is a key word in that. In 1922 (the year in which the story of *The Great Gatsby* took place), there were middle-class residential communities, with gas stations, dime stores, neighborhood movies, and offices on Long Island—but Nick ignores all that. To him, the whole island was made riotous by the behavior of the rich, and we begin to get a sense of place as Nick sees it.

The sense of place gathers in everything: the mountains or plains, the deserts or the streets of a town, the quality of life, people's manners, dress, morals, religion, commerce, and so on. In her small book *Place in Fiction*, Eudora Welty observes that "it is by the nature of itself that fiction is all bound up in the local. The internal reason for that is surely that feelings are bound up in places. . . . Location is the crossroads of circumstance, the proving ground of 'What happened? Who's here? Who's coming?'" She adds, "The sense of a story when the visibility [i.e., the setting] is only partial or intermittent is as endangered as Eliza crossing the ice."

In the hands of some writers, place declines from its role as part of a total vision and becomes heavy furnishings—or the "furniture" of fiction that Willa Cather so deplored. It is used in the hope of achieving authority by sheer mass of detail; it is like a Victorian parlor, so crowded with red plush, fringes, horsehair, ferns, gilt frames, brass, and keepsakes that it is hard to see what is going on in the midst of all that. The opposite failure seems common in current fiction. During the heyday of the regional novel, writers could spend a lifetime immersed in a province of their own. There were the widely known writers such as Faulkner, Ellen Glasgow, Willa Cather, and Sherwood Anderson as well as the lesser-known such as Sarah Orne Jewett, Ruth Suckow, O. E. Rölvaag, Jessamyn West, and Conrad Richter. Now, in a culture that has been much homogenized by travel, television, and education, the idea of region as a special place apart has become more a thing of the legendary past. Regional fiction is likely to be set at least a generation ago. In a novel like Olive Ann Burns's *Cold Sassy Tree* (1985), the reader must accept the author's assurance that things in the not-so-long-ago remained much as they always used to be. The regional novel used to view change as a matter of replacing the sod hut or log cabin with the clapboard house or the brick dwelling, the dusty village with the thriving town. Today, it is a change in the whole fabric of life. A lot of the young people have left to live in the city; the family farms round about are being sold and agribusiness is taking over; everybody watches television and there are no more band concerts in the park or amateur theatricals—even the movie house is closed; the kids all go to a consolidated high school five miles away; you can't even get to Davenport on the train any longer.

John Gardner believes that the coming of a more homogeneous culture has made young writers see derivatively: "Much of the dialogue one encounters in student fiction, as well as plot, gesture, even setting, come not from life but from life filtered through TV. Many student writers seem unable to tell their own most important stories—the death of a father, the first disillusionment in love—except in the molds and formulas of TV. And . . . TV is false to life." Of course, all writers are derivative in a certain way—but it used to be that the young writer derived his plot, gesture, and setting from the kind of stories Aunt Em used to tell in front of the fireplace after supper or, elsewhere, the ones Uncle Isidore told as we sat on the brownstone front steps on a summer evening. The writer-to-be was breathing his environment, hearing it, and seeing it around him. That is why America has produced so much good regional fiction—which of course includes what we often think of as "ethnic" fiction. The Jewish community on the Lower East Side, the Greek neighborhood in Chicago, and Irish South Boston are just as much regions of America as Yoknapatawpha County.

It is true that these locales have lost some of their peculiarly regional ways and subject matter, but people still go on living in particular houses, on particular streets in particular towns where they share an outlook, an accent, a history, and certain myths with the people around them. That setting, as Eudora Welty writes, goes on exercising a "delicate control" over their character. Much has been lost, but a good writer can show us how much still remains.

In the next section, we look at some of the good and bad uses of background and setting.

PICTURE POSTCARDS

Writers whose fiction stays at home are far less likely to gather irrelevant and stereotypical detail than those who go traveling. The writer in transit will often pick up the picture-postcard and tour-guide kind of information that is sometimes called "local color." They miss the less-obvious tenor of daily life unique to any place. A good example of a bad example is a story by Sarah Orne Jewett, an excellent and rather underrated writer of the latter half of the nineteenth century. Sarah Jewett was a bred-in-the-bone Down East Yankee and Maine was her country, but once she was tempted to try an Old South story, which she called "The Mistress of Sydenham Plantation." (She once said that when an old lady and a house came together in her mind, the result was a story.)

The time is in the 1880s, some twenty-odd years after Mrs. Sydenham's husband and sons were killed in the Civil War, but she is convinced that they are still alive and the war is still going on. On the day before Easter, she decides to visit the family plantation on St. Helena Island to make sure that its great house is ready for the family's annual move. Her old manservant tries to dissuade her because he is afraid that the sight of the ruined house will kill her, but she will not listen. When she arrives, "The crumbled, fallen chimneys of the house were there among the weeds, and that was all." But what Mrs. Sydenham sees is the old mansion still in all its splendor.

In the crisp, cold air of Maine, Sarah Jewett is crisp and exact. In the sultry air of the Sea Islands, she goes misty and superficial. Notice all the false touches in this reportage (the italics are ours):

In the *quaint* churchyard of old St. Helena's church . . . the gravestones themselves were moss-grown and *ancient-looking;* yet here and there the *wounded look* of the earth *appealed to the eye,* and *betrayed* a new-made grave. The old sarcophagi and the heavy tablets of the historic Beaufort families stood side by side with plain wooden crosses. The *armorial bearings* and the long epitaphs of the one and the brief lettering of the other suggested the changes that had come with the war to these families, yet somehow the wooden *cross touched one's heart with closer sympathy. . . . The five doors of the church* were standing open. On the steps of that *eastern door, which opened midway up the side aisle,* where the morning sun had shown upon the *white faces of a hospital in war-time. . . .*

She was a very stately *gentlewoman,* for one so small and thin . . . but there was a true elegance and dignity in the way she moved, and those who saw her—*persons who shuffled when they walked and boasted loudly of the fallen pride of the South*— were *struck* with a *sudden deference and admiration.*[1]

We can almost see the author taking notes: "Church has five doors, eastern one opens halfway up aisle. Used as hospital during war—recall white faces of wounded as sun comes in through door and falls on them. . . ." The church, of course, has nothing to do with the story, but it makes a very picturesque postcard. Mrs. Sydenham herself is something of a postcard, although it seems unlikely that touring Yankees were "struck with a sudden deference and admiration" for this elderly lady who had been slightly bonkers for twenty years.

Although the message side of a postcard is mercifully brief, the cards are cheap and a writer with a little time to waste can send a lot of them. He will want us to know everything of what he has been seeing. His excessive detail proves that he has been paying attention in the daytime and reading Baedecker in his room at night. A good working rule for any writer, however, is to consider how much of the acquired knowledge has a bearing on the story. Sinclair Lewis, new to the subject, once tried to write a novel about the life of hotelkeepers and only succeeded in writing a beginner's manual for the occupation.

When the story or novel requires some close description of its setting, the writer will be wise to distribute the scenery bit by bit throughout the story. That nice touch about the old stone wall with the climbing roses here and that view of the house at the end of the village street a little later—but only if they have a place in the story. And, even though it took hours of research in the library, is that description of the Indian mounds outside of town really relevant? As Elizabeth Bowen said, "The weak novelist is always, compensatorily, scene-minded."

And Chekhov said, "Descriptions should be very brief and have an incidental nature." He thought that the best method was to "snatch at small details, grouping them in such a manner that after reading them, one can obtain the picture on closing one's eyes." A moonlit night could be evoked by writing, "On the mill-dam a sliver of broken bottle flashed like a small, bright star, and there rolled by . . . the black shadow of a dog, or a wolf."

Suppose, though, that a writer does have ample reason for telling a good deal about his setting, and he asks, "Should I intersperse layers of action and layers of description as if I were making a club sandwich?"

In such a case, description should be mingled with action—not just the physical action of the story but its mental and emotional activity as well. "Scene can only be justified," says Elizabeth Bowen, "where it has dramatic use." *A Passage to India* contains an immense amount of Indian sound, smell, sight, and impression, but it is so carefully blended into the lives of the characters that it never strikes the reader as irrelevant tourism:

> As the elephant moved toward the hills . . . a new quality occurred, a spiritual silence which invaded more senses than the ear. Life went on as usual, but had no consequences, that is to say, sounds did not echo or thoughts develop. Everything seemed cut off at the root, and therefore infected with illusion. For instance, there were some mounds by the edge of the track, low, serrated, and touched with whitewash. What were these mounds—graves, breasts of the goddess Parvati? The villagers beneath gave both replies. Again, there was a confusion about a snake which was never cleared up. Miss Quested saw a thin, dark object reared on end at the further side of a watercourse, and said, "A snake!" The villagers agreed, and Aziz explained: yes, a black cobra, very venomous, who had reared himself up to watch the passing of the elephant. But when she looked through Ronny's field glasses, she found it was . . . the withered and twisted stump of a toddy palm.[2]

Not all writers are as subtle as Forster, and there can be other ways of justifying a density of detail. The "naturalistic" novelists, whose line began a little over a hundred years ago with such writers as Émile Zola and descended through Arnold Bennett in England and Theodore Dreiser in America, had an obsession with the details of social milieus. They wanted to write about the "real world." That meant that they did not think much about private worlds where values might be concerned with love, charity, friendship, loyalty, and with art, literature, music, and the love of nature.

Sometimes openly and sometimes in what Mark Schorer calls "buried metaphor," they dwelt on money coming in and going out, the values of properties, good and bad investments, legal proceedings, the manufacture of things and their markets. Others were concerned with workers' lives and working conditions, the difficulties of making ends meet when owners keep wages low and profits high, the politics of capitalism and socialism. To convince the reader of these realities, they packed in plenty of researched detail—with the result that they are not very widely read in this later time.

Another trouble that writers today sometimes get into is the use of place as a kind of collection of clichés. It is not the same thing as local colorism; rather, it is a matter of taking the known and familiar aspects of a place and remaking them into a popular product for export. In what might be called Norman Rockwell-izing, the landscape, customs, attitudes, and habits of speech in some fictional province are made quaint and colorful. Anglo-Irish writers used to exploit the Irish peasantry this way, making them appear cheerfully dishonest, always avoiding work, full of superstition and strong drink. We have had our own examples, such as DuBose Heyward's *Porgy* (made into an opera as *Porgy and Bess*) and many books about the folks in Appalachia. There is even a touch of it in Steinbeck's novels about migrant field-workers.

For contrast, one might consider a novel such as John Fowles's *The French Lieutenant's Woman*. Although, with its mingling of present and past, it is not a conventional regional novel, it does recreate the Victorian world of Lyme Regis in a convincing way. In quite another mode, there is Carolyn Chute's 1985 novel *The Beans of Egypt, Maine,* a remarkable picture of life in poverty in rural Maine. It does not sample well, but here is a passage that gives some slight flavor of the story:

> Since the stroke, Earlene knows Gram's body by heart. She rubs her with cornstarch every morning and arranges her in the wheelchair in her new violet print dress or one of the other dresses, always steam-ironed. Tied to one armrest is a loud silver bell, which Gram rings if Earlene gets too far off in the house.
>
> Earlene's small wallpapered bedroom is upstairs. She leaves the door open at night and imagines every sound is Gram's bell.[3]

One of the writer's best possessions is the place he knows, but without reverence for the truth about this place, he can make it into a stage set. It has been said that traditions are those things a society pretends to honor but no longer observes. This should apply not only to manners, customs, and beliefs but to ways of looking at the physical landscape. The serious writer will view all these with an unsentimental, modern-day vision.

The most common problem in trying to create a setting is far less the problem of exaggerating its clichés (quaint, ugly, poverty-stricken, violent, or whatever) than that of making it vivid to the reader. Thomas Hardy was so successful at this that his invented county of Wessex in southern England came to be accepted by readers as a real place. Hardy noted that "the appellation which I had thought to reserve to the

horizons and landscapes of a partly-real, partly-dream country has become more and more popular as a practical provin-
cial definition; and the dream-country has, by degrees,
solidified into a utilitarian region which people can go to, take
a house in, and write to the papers from." He added, "I will
ask all good and idealistic readers . . . to refuse steadfastly
to believe that there are any inhabitants of a Victorian Wessex
outside these volumes in which their lives and conversations
are detailed."

Powerful fictions have always had this transforming
effect on geography—Trollope's Barsetshire is another example—and it is hard to think of Salem without Hawthorne's
perception of it; the Hudson Valley is flavored with recollections of Washington Irving; and we can see Chicago through
the eyes of Saul Bellow. Mrs. Gaskell, in her biography of
Charlotte Brontë, has left a striking account of the difference
between a fictional reality and a mere temporal actuality. She
visited Haworth and the country around it in 1855, less than
a decade after *Wuthering Heights* and *Jane Eyre* were written
there and found "villas, great worsted factories, rows of work-
men's houses . . . it can hardly be called 'country' any part
of the way." To the west of the village, Mrs. Gaskell does give
us a glimpse of "dun and purple moors." But can this be the
"wild moorland," the "remote, unreclaimed region" Emily
Brontë beheld?

True, *Wuthering Heights* is technically a historical novel,
taking place largely in the last quarter of the eighteenth
century, but can anyone doubt that the landscape we see
through the eyes of Lockwood (who narrates much of the
book) is the one that Emily was convinced she looked out on?

The writer's great obligation is to make the reader visualize a place from a single, intense viewpoint capable of filtering out the worsted factories, rows of workers' houses, and the villas.

SOME USES OF DETAIL

If he wants effective detail, the writer must have these (earlier noted) taboos in mind: (1) irrelevant or picture-postcard detail; (2) excess; (3) visual, ethnic, linguistic, or other clichés; (4) derivative, secondhand material. In trying to refine his perception to just the details that are both deeply characteristic of a place and relevant to the action of his story, he must know first precisely what role the surroundings are to carry out.

Not every story or novel, of course, has an intimacy with its setting. For one thing, in this mobile and restless age, most characters will not stay put. They go on journeys, take jobs in another part of the country or the world, or have missions of some kind. Then there are the characters who are more or less oblivious to their surroundings for whatever reason. It then becomes an authorial responsibility to sketch the world around them—but without letting the characters know it. Again, the author who sets his story in some unfamiliar time and/or place, must slip in the details his characters would take for granted. He has to create a selected verisimilitude somewhere in between the naturalistic novelist's long catalogs and inventories and the Elizabethan playwright's sign appearing on a bare stage: A FOREST NEAR GLOUCESTER CASTLE.

There is nothing really wrong with making the locale no

more than a backdrop for a story—if it is that kind of a story. In this case, the Elizabethan playwright was perfectly justified. His characters were not going to have to make camp in the forest, gather wood, build fires, dig a latrine, find a water supply—neither were they going to interest themselves in the ecological system of the forest or the lives of the birds and animals within it. They were concerned with working out some drama of love or intrigue among themselves, one that might have taken place almost anywhere.

Broadly speaking, there are five primary functions for place or setting.

1. Place as character.
2. Place as destiny.
3. Place as narrative element.
4. Place as period.
5. Place as backdrop.

"Place as character" is an unsatisfactory phrase and, as the reader will understand, it does not mean that a locale should be given human traits or personality. "Place as character" means that the setting affects the people in a story as much as they affect one another. They are subject to its weather, hazards, beguilements, confinements, and temperature. What results is a kind of interaction between place and person— as, in a broader sense, the Swiss character is conditioned by a land of high mountains and deep valleys. At its most powerful, fiction with this element commands our affections as well as our imagination in a way that other novels and stories do not. The reason is that—for a great many readers, at least—

"feelings are bound up in places," as Eudora Welty points out.

There is, however, one very great difficulty that the writer faces when he chooses to celebrate his setting—if he departs from it, he risks his reader's disbelief. Within the author's own territory, we accept almost anything that happens. But let anyone in the story take a car or a plane to alien parts and the power of illusion may be lost. The thing that is wrong with Willa Cather's *A Lost Lady* is Marian Forrester's reappearance in Buenos Aires long years after her disgrace and disappearance from Sweet Water. Her triumph in South America is quite as improbable as her being there at all. Her vanities, gaieties, transgressions, and assumed sophistication are effective and moving only when confined to "one of those gray towns along the Burlington railroad" and to that house "well known from Omaha to Denver for its hospitality and for a certain charm of atmosphere." The novel should have ended with Marian's going away. That it doesn't is an example of Willa Cather's curiously deficient aesthetic sensibility and—more to our present point—an example of how easily even veteran writers can go wrong. William Maxwell made the same error with a final, unnecessary chapter in *The Folded Leaf.* In a reprint of the book, he wisely decided to delete this chapter, finishing the story in the place and among the people where it had developed.

Place as character is closely linked with place as destiny. The human characters are condemned by their environment to certain fates. Much of the drama emerges from the differences between, for example, what the Emma Bovarys or Carol Kennicotts long for and what their world will let them have.

Sometimes place offers a benign or, at least, tolerable destiny—as in Frank O'Connor's stories of western Ireland —but authors are usually attracted to the greater drama of people in revolt against their circumambience or defeated by it. Contented people, unfortunately, tend to be somewhat boring.

American fiction about men and women as victims of their environment usually concerns people trapped in bad jobs, bad country, or bad obligations—Willa Cather's characters who detest Nebraska, Robert Penn Warren's who feel doomed in the South, all of the women in stories who are condemned to care for invalid mothers or fathers. These hardships pale beside those of Aleksandr Solzhenitsyn's characters, who are prisoners of their surroundings in the bleakest and most literal sense. Two of his powerful novels—*One Day in the Life of Ivan Denisovich* and *The First Circle*— are stories of the Gulag, Russian concentration camps. Another, *The Cancer Ward*, is explained by its title. An environment of hate, repression, coercion so total is almost beyond the American imagination; compare the girl looking out the window at wintry Nebraska fields and longing to go to the crowded excitement of the big city with the girl looking past the barbed wire at the Siberian steppes and longing for *any-place* else in the world. As Solzhenitsyn (in *The Cancer Ward*) says:

Only a prisoner in his first years of sentence believes, every time he is summoned from his cell and told to collect his belongings, that he is being called to freedom. To him every whisper of an amnesty sounds like the trumpets of archangels. But they call him out of his cell, read him some loathsome documents and shove him into another cell on the floor below, even darker than the previous one but with the same stale used-up air.

The cells of the heart which nature built for joy die through misuse. That small place in the breast which is faith's cramped quarters stays without tenant for years and decays from disuse.[4]

The ideas of place as character and place as destiny get their force from the terrible history of the twentieth century, when much of mankind has lived in confinement by tyrants or totalitarian regimes. For a great many people, the state itself is the character and destiny of the world in which they live.

When place is employed as merely one more narrative element, it will not govern those large questions that every serious fiction proposes. It will have little effect on choice and it will probably not limit possibility. It will neither enhance nor impair human dignity, courage, conviction, or love. In short, it is milieu, the setting in which the fiction happens to occur.

It was the fourth week of the Oxford summer term. . . . It was Eights Week, when the colleges raced their boats to determine which college should be Head of the River. Francis . . . was having a very important conversation with Ismay in the open air, sitting comfortably on the upper deck of the Corpus barge, amid a din of cheering, as they ate strawberries and cream and watched the sweating oarsmen.[5]

For Robertson Davies's purpose, the details provide a sufficient setting for the conversation that takes place between the central character in *What's Bred in the Bone* and his girl-friend. We never learn anything more about the boat race or the barge in which the young man and woman are sitting.

A more imaginative use of milieu appears in John Up-dike's short story "How to Love America and Leave it at the Same Time"—in fact, it could be said that milieu is the subject of the story.

An unnamed narrator and his family are traveling by car in California:

Arrive in some town around three, having been on the road since seven, and cruise the main street, which is also Route Whatev-er-It-Is, and vote on the motel you want. The wife favors a discreet back-from-the-road look, but not bungalows; the kids go for a pool (essential), color TV (optional), and Magic Fingers (fun). Vote with the majority, pull in, and walk to the office. Your legs unbend weirdly after all that sitting behind the wheel. A sticker on the door says the place is run by "The Plummers," so this is Mrs. Plummer behind the desk. Fifty-fiveish, tight silver curls with traces of copper, face moth-erly but for the brightness of the lipstick and the sharpness of the sizing-up glance.

Say the town is in California, on the dry side of the Sierras; though it could as well be in Iowa, or Kentucky, or Connecticut.

Or, alternatively, get into the car at the motel and drive around the back streets: a wooden church, a brick elementary school with basketball stanchions on a pond of asphalt, houses spaced and square-set and too clean-looking. . . . But the kids are bored and beg to go "home." Home is the motel.

Where shall we eat? Discuss. . . . Perhaps the kids win, and you sit there looking out through the windows thinking, This is

America, a hamburger kingdom, one cuisine under God, indivisible, with pickles and potato chips for all.[6]

In effect, Updike is saying that much of America is one big milieu. In our life of travel and transit, we can pass from one town to an interchangeable next. The houses, the traffic, the hamburgers are quite the same everywhere and the only home is the motel—for the moment.

When it comes to providing background for characters who are oblivious to their surroundings, Alberto Moravia found a good solution—although it is not one that will work in every instance. In *The Empty Canvas*, he uses, for his purpose, a Curious Questioner named Dino, a young man who is infatuated with a beautiful girl from a stratum of Roman society unknown to him:

"You live in a flat in the Prati district?"
"Yes."
"How many rooms have you?'
"I don't know."
"What d'you mean, you don't know?"
"I've never counted them."
"But is it a big or small flat?"
"So-so."
"What does that mean?"
"Medium-sized."
"Well then, describe it."[7]

Henry James employed the *ficelle*, or confidant, in order to convey information that the "central intelligence" of the story could not plausibly find out for himself. The Curious Questioner can play a similar role when the author is trying to develop a background for some character who is unaware that such a thing exists. In *The Empty Canvas*, Moravia is able to use this frustrating dialogue to move to a development of the story. Dino, in an agony of curiosity, is finally driven to go to see the girl's home for himself. Such an action is contrary to what we know of Dino's ordinary behavior, but Moravia makes us believe it as evidence of the young man's mounting obsession for everything connected with the girl.

When description is used to establish the period of a story, the writer may find that a straightforward approach is not only the simplest but most effective. At the beginning of his novel *Legs* (one of the Albany novels), William Kennedy has to establish the period as the 1920s. He does it by giving us some headline notes on his main character:

> I had come to see Jack as not merely the dude of all gangsters, the most active brain in the New York underworld, but as one of the truly new American Irishmen of his day; Horatio Alger out of Finn McCool and Jesse James, shaping the dream that you could grow up in America and shoot your way to glory and riches. . . . He was almost as famous as Lindbergh while his light burned. "The Most Picturesque Racketeer in the Underworld," the New York *American* called him; "Most Publicized of Public Enemies," said the *Post*. "Most Shot-At Man in America," said the *Mirror*.[8]

At the beginning of Scott Fitzgerald's story "Babylon Revisited," there are subtler signals to suggest the period:

He was not really disppointed to find Paris was so empty. But the stillness in the Ritz bar was strange and portentous. It was not an American bar any more—he felt polite in it, and not as if he owned it. It had gone back into France.

Charlie directed his taxi to the Avenue de l'Opéra, which was out of his way. But he wanted to see the blue hour spread over the magnificent facade, and imagine that the cab horns, endlessly playing the first few bars of *"Le Plus que Lent,"* were the trumpets of the Second Empire. They were closing the iron grill in front of Brentano's bookstore, and people were already at dinner behind the trim little bourgeois hedge of Duval's. He had never eaten at a really cheap restaurant in Paris. Five course dinner, four francs fifty, eighteen cents, wine included.[9]

It takes a little—but not very much—knowledge of the 1920s to know that the Ritz Hotel bar was the great rendezvous of Americans at that time and that the Americans largely disappeared after the stock market crash of 1929. And, too, one has never been able to dine at a Paris restaurant for eighteen cents since those distant days.

Finally, certain writers prefer to use place as no more than a backdrop. The difference between milieu and backdrop is that milieu is just a place—everybody's Manhattan Upper West Side neighborhood or everybody's new Milwaukee suburb. The characters did not grow up there, they have no interest in it, and whatever personality of its own it might have is never noticed in the story, let alone having an effect on the characters in any way. But the characters are, nevertheless, solidly in the middle of it. Its geography is real.

The backdrop, on the other hand, is obviously make-believe. It might be the nameless and featureless big city, the seacoast summer resort, or the country. Its only reason for being mentioned at all is because we know that people live in places, and so there has to be a somewhere. In Ann Beattie's very good novel *Falling in Place*, the stage-set suburbia could be any suburbia, although the author is thoughtful enough to tell us that it's in Connecticut. This is about as much as she wishes to tell us about the surroundings:

> John Joel was high up in the tree. . . . The robins had left their nest early in the week, so John Joel had his favorite resting place back: the tenth branch up, the one that he could crawl out on, high above his mother's Chevy and the small, kidney-shaped pool, now empty, that in previous summers had held goldfish, tadpoles, and water lilies, and now was filled with sticks and leaves no one had cleared out when winter ended.[10]

The important thing for Ann Beattie is her network of stories about a variety of discontented people—who are detached from the place where they just happen to live.

In the end, there are no rules about the uses of place in fiction—there are only the individual propensities of authors. Some see and feel every glint, texture, and noise of the world around them, and so they cannot imagine a story that happens almost nowhere, or that happens in front of a stage set. Other writers are so concerned with human subjects—"the proper study of mankind is man"—that they shut out the great, distracting buzz of natural or man-made worlds. On one hand we have the Yorkshire moorlands, on the other the nearly anonymous Metropolis where so much American fictional life is now lived.

Notes to Chapter 6

1. From *Strangers and Wayfarers* (Boston: Houghton Mifflin Co., 1890), pp. 18–21.
2. New York: Harcourt, Brace & Co., 1924; pp. 140–41.
3. New York: Ticknor & Fields, 1985; p. 120.
4. Nicholas Bethell and David Burg, trans. (New York: Farrar, Straus & Giroux, 1969), p. 263.
5. New York: Viking Press, 1985; pp. 244–45.
6. From *Problems* (New York: Alfred A. Knopf, 1979), pp. 40, 44, 45.
7. Angus Davidson, trans. (New York: Farrar, Straus & Giroux, 1961), pp. 154–55.
8. New York: Coward, McCann & Geoghegan, 1975; p. 13.
9. From *The Stories of F. Scott Fitzgerald* (New York: Charles Scribner's Sons, 1951), pp. 385, 386.
10. New York: Random House, 1980; p. 3.

SEVEN

NARRATIVE STYLE: TIME AND PACE IN FICTION

SCENE AND NARRATION

"Oh, pardon!" Shakespeare asked his audience; pardon for the violence that every storyteller since time began has had to do to time and space. "Can this cockpit hold / The vasty fields of France? or may we cram / Within this wooden O the very casques / That did affright the air at Agincourt?" In fact, of course not. But then, by the special laws of relativity that operate within any fiction, of course it can. One crooked figure can, in little space, stand for a million; whole kingdoms can rise; thoughts can deck out kings and "Carry them here and there, jumping o'er times, / Turning the accomplishments of many years / Into an hourglass. . . ." And just because the author does have this power to compress, expand, select, to range over time and space, he must use it with the greatest skill and greatest advantage to his story.

The two problems, what might be called the Problem of the Wooden O and the Problem of the Hour Glass, can be discussed together because they are interdependent. Both of them are closely connected with the important matter of pace in fiction.

That is, each story or novel has a special pace of development, hurrying at times and slowing at others. The writer judges at which point he will proceed deliberately, giving us the story detail by detail, almost at the speed with which the action might have taken place, and at what point he will pass quickly over a stretch of time, reporting only the general sequence of events. In between these two extremes, there can be other, varying tempos called for.

Good storytellers have always known when to slow pace and when to quicken it. " 'Now let us discuss this matter,' said the Caliph to his prisoner. He motioned for the guards to withdraw and the man seated himself cross-legged in front of the dais where the Caliph sat. . . ." is the opposite extreme of "Ten years passed while the exiled Caliph wandered from camp to camp in the desert or village to village on the plains."

The traditional rule is that all episodes meant to show important behavior in the characters, to make events dramatic as in theater, or to bring news that changes the situation should be dealt with in the scenic, or eyewitness, manner. Stretches of time or occurrences that are secondary to the story's development are handled by means of what is called a "narrative bridge."

The writer manages to be invisible and unheard during his slow, detailed observation in the scenic mode. He sits, watches, and records. He can look at the furnishings of the room (or the features of the landscape) with as much care as he likes. He can examine his characters from head to foot. He can note the clues of their "silent language," which is made up of gesture, expression, position, attitude. Above all, he can listen to them talk. While he may summarize indirectly the less important things being said, he will let us hear most of this word for word. He does not select on the basis of mere relevance; the object is to try to persuade the reader that he is listening to the flow of talk on which the story, at this moment, is being carried. If the story happens to be told from the definite point of view of one person, the invisible reporter can look through that person's eyes at what is going on and apprehend the scene as colored by the character's thoughts, emotions, or prejudices.

Here is an example from a short story titled "Gaps" by Ann Beattie:

She's giggling, driving too fast on purpose, to confuse him. He hates her when she's this way.

"And do you know what she told my mother? She said that the day the Apollo spacecraft landed on the moon Wesley wouldn't leave the television set, even to eat."

"What's so funny about that?"

She's steering with her left hand, and she's right-handed. There's a yellow warning sign, but she's going too fast to notice.

"Some people don't laugh in the face of progress," he adds, gripping the dashboard.

"Wait, let me tell it." She's looking at him instead of the road. "So later that afternoon Mrs. Dutton heard Wesley pacing. She looked in his bedroom and there he was, walking around with two big squares of foam rubber tied under his shoes."

Why did he agree to this ride? Every time the car cuts around a curve, he's sure he's going to die.[1]

Fiction that does not create this kind of immediacy can have a remote and hearsay quality. The scenic mode gives an author the chance to focus sharply, to close in on his subject; and when it is handled well, it gives the story a magical illusion of living and breathing life present at the very moment before the reader's eyes. Just because it is so splendid a technical chance, it should never be squandered.

It can be squandered by writing scenes that follow a serpentine course without ever seeming to point toward a meaning. Two notable American novelists guilty of this at times were Theodore Dreiser and—for example, in *The Ambassadors*—Henry James. The mistake comes from too much straining after reality. It may stem from James's desire to have his characters explain everything they think or feel at the moment, in extenso. A recent and much more egregious example is Scott Spencer's popular 1979 novel, *Endless Love*. There is unconscious irony in the title, because one scene between the hero and a woman prolongs small talk and sexual experiments over the space of fifty-two pages.

After a certain amount of time, the reader begins to realize that this kind of narration is less the work of an author than an unedited film. In a story of this sort, the telephone rings but it is a wrong number; Jane starts to light a cigarette but thinks better of it; Michael tells a joke but forgets the punch line. All the irrelevance is left in just to prove—what? A power of total recall, perhaps.

Now being irrelevant, or apparently irrelevant, for the moment can be one of the beauties of fiction. Chekhov did that for special effects of comedy or suspense. Nikolai Gogol did it with a syntactical sleight-of-hand. As Vladimir Nabokov notes in his book about Gogol, "We are faced with the phenomenon of mere forms of speech directly giving rise to live creatures."

He then quotes from *Dead Souls:* "Even the weather had obligingly accommodated itself to the setting: the day was neither bright nor gloomy but a kind of bluey-gray tint such as is found only in the worn-out uniforms of garrison soldiers, for the rest a peaceful class of warrior except for their being somewhat inebriate on Sundays." Nabokov observes that "for the rest" (or *vprochem* in Russian) is a false link that transits from a sunless landscape to a groggy old soldier accosting the reader with a rich hiccup on the festive outskirts of the sentence.

But irrelevancy cannot lead to more irrelevancy. Some line of logic must be progressing in the scene and some addition to the pattern must be developing.

To avoid such troubles, the beginning writer can follow a useful logic. He can start by thinking of the scene he is about to write as a short act in a drama. First of all, it is to be self-contained and to produce its own definite meanings. These meanings must, however, contribute something of value to the total meaning of the fiction. The "act" or dramatic passage, therefore, must have a shape to it. It must have a beginning, a development, and a result. It may make several (but not too many) interesting points as it proceeds, but it must always aim toward a culmination that justifies the scene's existence. The meaning may be large or small, of either incidental importance or crucial importance, open to the reader immediately or with a deferred significance. It may be quite explicit or it may be symbolical. The important thing is that it is put before the reader's eyes dramatically—thus, it is far more emphatic and immediate than a narrative statement could be. The reader has a chance to participate in the story; he sees certain evidence and forms certain conclusions; his intelligence has been engaged; he is working out the implicit, the unspoken, side of the story. He knows, of course, that the result is foregone and that the sense of working it out is an illusion, but it is one of the most potent illusions any writer can create.

It is a principle of high importance that the truly significant ideas arise from some viewed interplay of life in a story rather than from flat statement. Saying "Steven was a vain and quite fatuous young man" is something different from hearing him talking about his clothes, name-dropping to impress people, and trying to get himself invited to the right dinner parties. In the first, the truth is a statistic; in the second, it is a deduction from observed evidence. This is as true of actions as of words. The interesting, revelatory, unpredictable actions that contribute most richly to story or character ought to be treated in process, as they gradually expose themselves in the scene.

A small but common mistake of writers—even good writers—is to tell the same thing in two different ways, by report and by demonstration. Dostoevsky interrupts one scene in *The Brothers Karamazov* to say, "But the Captain was to have his hopes cruelly dashed." He then goes on to show the captain having just that disappointment in the scene. The remark, of course, should not be made by the author but by the reader—and at the end of the scene: "Aha, I can see that the captain has had his hopes, etc., etc." It would be an equal mistake to describe "the judge with a mouth that looked like an old knife-scar and cruel blue eyes—a man who seemed capable of automatic injustice" and then to go into a scene showing him living up to his description. The scene has then become an anecdote to adorn the initial generalization. The reader has been told rudely what to think, the dramatic continuity has been interrupted, and the scenic demonstration of the judge's character has become anticlimactic. In both these cases, the writer confesses either a lack of faith in his audience—they will not be able to deduce for themselves—or a lack of faith in his own ability—he does not believe that he can show without telling.

When to move quickly over stretches of uninteresting time is a decision that needs careful thought. "Galloway took a taxi at La Guardia and went to the World Trade Center." That sentence gets him there and tells us that nothing significant happened on the way. "With the passage of years, Helen was able to forget her sorrow." The story has been moved from one point to a new phase. "Later that summer, Hans Packard died, and George suddenly found himself rich enough to buy out his partner in the business and make it his own, even though Maria took legal action to try to break the will." That sentence spans a series of predictable events that do not have to be treated in any detail.

A primitive kind of storytelling puts a great deal—or all —of the work in the form of narrative summary like the examples above. The modern tendency is to use this kind of summary much more sparingly. A great many successful modern short stories are entirely scenic; there seems to be something old-fashioned about one that drops into narrative summary for long. The twenty-four-hour novel has had a vogue—Joyce's *Ulysses* being the most prominent example. A novel such as Saul Bellow's *Humboldt's Gift* moves from scene to scene with an elision that makes narrative bridges almost unnecessary. Even today, however, there will be certain points that demand putting months or years into the hourglass of language so that the story can move quickly forward.

This kind of condensation of time in summary should be subsequent to, and derive from, a scenic part of the story. The dramatic scene has developed event, interest in character, and almost all of the tension, and the narrative will roll along on that momentum. After Mr. A's good-bye scene with his wife, the reader now has enough interest to follow him as he leaves his hotel, takes a taxi to the airport, makes a dash to his boarding gate, and manages to board just before the flight takes off. There was a time when most readers would be curious about the details of this; nowadays everybody has gone through just this action himself or herself or has seen it on television. It is no news to the reader and so it needs no detailed description—unless, of course, something noteworthy happens on that short trip. If so, there may be a couple of moments worth noting. In the taxi, A reflects on the bitter argument he has had with his wife just before leaving. Then, at the baggage check-in counter, there is a brief disagreement with a man who is rushing for another plane and who insists on thrusting his bags onto the scales along with Mr. A's. Mr. A is very rude in return. Though his trip to the airport has told us nothing substantive, we are beginning to get a sense of what he is like.

The narrative summary can be used to point toward the next dramatic development; it can set the scene or indicate the next stage of action. It can imply or drop clues, but it should not be given the job of developing the plot or story.

It is only when Mr. A arrives in London and goes to his hotel, perhaps, that we revert to the scenic way of looking at things. Say that we slow down to scenic time as we watch him open his bags and begin to unpack. Horrors! Here is a large double-breasted suit with broad pin stripes, a purple bathrobe, and three pink shirts—the clothes of a large, loud stranger. He looks at the suitcase and sees that it is like his own but is not his. The recent suspicions he has had of his wife come back in a rush. Mr. A turns toward the telephone, and then he suddenly thinks of the other passenger who had insisted on pushing his bag onto the scales along with his own.

Narrative summary may not be merely utilitarian. It can be a vehicle for an author's generalizations about his scene or story and it can be nicely impressionistic. Here is an example from Carson McCullers' *The Ballad of the Sad Café:*

That autumn was a happy time. The crops around the countryside were good, and over at the Forks Falls market the price of tobacco held firm that year. After the long hot summer the first cool days had a clean bright sweetness. Goldenrod grew along the dusty roads and the sugar cane was ripe and purple. . . . Boys hunted foxes in the pinewoods, winter quilts were aired out on the wash lines and sweet potatoes bedded in the straw against the colder months to come.[2]

The "dramatic illusion" of a scene is so fragile that any interruption can break the spell, but narrative is coarser and rougher stuff. Episodes or a little dialogue can be patched in as the writer wishes. "Three days later, Chris picked up the phone to call Julie. He had even made pencilled notes on the confessions he would make before he asked her to forgive him.

" 'Hello,' she said. 'Who's this?' He looked at his notes. It suddenly struck him again that she was the one who was in the wrong—stubbornly, blindly, unreasonably. 'Wrong number, sorry,' he said."

This is a fleeting incident, not important enough to warrant a scene yet interesting enough to mention as an episode. The long stride of the narrative is slowed for a minute and we get a scenic glimpse and hear a voice or two. A number of things—generalization, description, episode, dialogue, etc. —can be used to break the monotonous tone of narrative summary and to give it a flexible, lively impression.

There is still the difficult question of which parts of the story deserve to be scenic and which do not—when to show or when to tell. Of course, different novels and stories make different demands, and there is no formula that will solve this problem neatly. Every author will have to survey his story's scheme and decide which portions suggest themselves as primary dramatic occurrences and which can be left to the schematic treatment of narrative. There will be places where the characters almost request the chance to appear as if on a stage, to voice their feelings and ideas and to act. These are the crucial moments in their lives. Most short stories are necessarily limited to crucial moments. The novelist has a different problem. He will want many of his scenes in a quieter key, scenes that may carry as much meaning as the more striking ones but that develop it more gradually and subtly. It is here that the decision as to what should be told in the dramatic mode becomes difficult.

It is here, too, that we have reached one of the borders between craft and art. There are some practical suggestions to be made, but it is finally artistic judgment that the writer must rely on in order to sense where his drama lies and where his narrative. As an illustration of this, there is a notable difference in national sensibilities between Nordic and Celtic.

In the Norse sagas, when the hero meets death in battle, the description of his dying is terse, cut off suddenly as was the warrior. In Irish tales and legends, the death of the hero is an occasion for stirring poetry, drawn-out final minutes, and lamentation. Death is stark, quick, and final—or death is life's final scene, with a grand, ceremonial exit called for. In the same way, two authors may see quite different answers to any problem of scene.

The best that a book on technique can offer are a few ideas on what usually works and what doesn't. The novelist has to think of the overall plan of his book. If he has brief scenes interspersed with long narrative stretches, he runs the danger of being tedious. If he tends to write many drawn-out scenes, he may lose their dramatic unity and their impact. It is unlikely that a novel whose first half is pure narrative and whose second half is pure scene would be successful; and just as unlikely that one whose beginning and end are scenic and whose middle stretch is all narrative would turn out well. In most novels, scene and narration succeed each other. Probably the most reliable approach is to work out a pattern of scenes for the entire book, one scene being followed by another of a contrasting kind, or several lesser scenes leading up to a big scene. Just the chore of writing this down might help the author to get an idea of the relationship of the parts in his "enacted" story.

In its primitive form, every piece of fiction first occurs to the mind as a little narrative. When the writer has that, he begins to hear his people speak and watch them act in certain situations. When he arranges these situations in some novelistic pattern, he has begun to create his scenario.

In good writing, there are no neat formulas, though. Most short stories and novels will go through many agonizing transformations in the course of being written—and, more important—being rewritten. Concepts will change and with them any preconceived pattern. Putting down a scenario is, nevertheless, good strategy that should warn the writer against scenes that are irrelevant, redundant, or in the wrong place. This plan also gives him a sense of how to pace the novel so that it does not seem to advance with jerky speed in one place and slow down to a crawl in another. Most useful of all, it makes him think hard about what should appear, as it were, onstage—in the foreground of his novel. Unlike a plot outline, the scene pattern is a way of deciding on the values given to each element in the story, how they are to be balanced in the design, and how they will succeed each other.

Among writers in English, Henry James was one of the great proponents of the "well-made novel," and he gave more attention to problems of pacing than most authors do. Explaining his method for *What Maisie Knew*, he said that the "treatment by scene regularly, quite rhythmically occurs." He noted that the "intervals between," or the narrative links, are all preparatory to the scenic occasions, and that the latter are "wholly and logically scenic," functioning as illustrations of his themes. He felt that the final success of the story rested on the fact that he had recognized the different responsibilities of scene and narrative.

By way of summing up, here are the various possible ways of pacing a story—short or long:

1. One scene alone that comprises the whole story.
2. Several separate scenes, with the transition from one to another noted briefly, but without any real narrative links.
3. Scene and narrative both used, succeeding each other as required throughout.
4. Narrative alone.

The first and second are the most popular methods among short story writers today and the third remains a reliable form for stories. Novelists use the second and third as standard methods but not the other two.

TIME AND HOW TO SHIFT IT

The element of time in fiction has so far been talked about almost wholly in terms of the pace at which the story proceeds, and we've assumed a simple chronological progression from event to event. A direct and narrow time line like that would be too confining for the modern writer; it belongs to the age of the straightforward tale. One of fiction's best inventions was the idea that the imagination is not ruled by clock and calendar. It comes from what Marcel Proust called "the inseparableness of us from the past"—the thought that something of our past is always with us and influencing us in each present moment. To use this, the novelist had to drop the classical rule of "unity of time" and to discover techniques for showing the presentness of the past in his story. And all of those techniques are relevant to something the critics call "enveloping action."

Enveloping action is the entire history of events that are relevant to the story—its past, its present, and its conceivable future. Of course, no fiction writer would ever want to deal with the whole scope, simply because his job as an artist is to choose the salient points in that long stretch of time and, by bringing these to life, create his story. The reader's attention is carefully guided to just the right hours of the past that demonstrate Proust's "inseparableness." As E. M. Forster observes, Proust could mesh two different times in his imagination so that "his hero was at the same period entertaining a mistress to supper and playing ball with his nurse in the park."

The most primitive kind of movement through fictional time is that device called the "flashback." Having reached a point where he sees a good chance to refer back, the author halts, puts up a notice as to where he's going, and flashes off: "When Moira pulled out the drawer, her eye fell on a snapshot of herself and Mark Barton half in sun, half in shadow, standing in front of some ruins. What ruins? Now she remembered and her mind went back to that incomparable summer of her nineteenth year on the island of Rhodes. . . ." The trouble with this ancient and trusty device is that it immediately announces itself as a device—as in an old movie when the screen is taken up by a calendar, its pages flipping backward frantically. The reader's willing suspension of disbelief gets a sharp jolt. Still, a feeble attempt at transition is better than no transition at all: "Moira sat down at her desk and began to remember. Ten years ago exactly she and Mark Barton had spent a joyful summer on the Greek island of Rhodes."

Used occasionally, the simple flashback does no great harm, but it becomes more obvious and awkward with repetition. For the writer who wishes to weave a number of past experiences into his present story, there must be a subtler, more inconspicuous method. The solution arrived at by some of the early twentieth-century writers (Marcel Proust, Henry James, Ford Madox Ford) was a technique that has been given the label of "the time-shift."

When the writer simply announces that he wishes to return to some bygone period, he seems to be arbitrary. He has to persuade the reader that the excursion is natural, even inevitable, in terms of the present story. One of the most effective ways of making the move is to go from the external scene and enter into the consciousness of the character who is providing the point of view. Thus far, there is no real difference from the example of the flashback given above. But, in the more sophisticated time-shift, phrases such as "her memory suddenly went back to the day when . . ." or "this reminded him of the time . . ." and similar sounds of counterclockwork are omitted. Instead, the author concentrates on writing a passage of seamless transition. Discreetly, he draws the reader's attention from the external scene in the present to something subjective—an abstraction or generalization from what has just been proceeding. Then, almost before the reader knows it, the abstract observation has led into another scene in another time.

An excellent example of this is shown in the opening passage of *Mrs. Dalloway,* quoted in the "Stream of Consciousness" section of chapter 4. Other smooth and artful uses of the time-shift appear in Ford Madox Ford's minor masterpiece *The Good Soldier,* in which it becomes a function of the whole fictional strategy. Ford uses time as a kind of montage, moving back and forth in it at will, making his present flow into the past and the past a ghostly part of the present. With utmost skill, he contrives never to finish one event or analysis of character before bringing in another, but always returning to what he has begun earlier in order to deepen it, give it a different cast, or to stress some new aspect.

In *The Good Soldier,* Leonora, wife of the British officer Edward Ashburnham, has an emotional breakdown. The narrator then proceeds to generalize about why this could have happened—he believes that she realizes that she can now trust her husband after years of tension and treachery. "And then," says the narrator, "with the slackening of her vigilance, came the slackening of her entire mind." This generalization suggests another. "You are to understand that Leonora loved Edward with a passion that was yet like an agony of hatred. And she had lived with him for years and years without addressing to him one word of tenderness."[3] At this point, the story is no longer inhabiting any actual moment in time—it is in some abstract area of the emotions—and, before we are quite aware that we have descended to earth again, we are with the nineteen-year-old Leonora in the garden of her father's run-down Irish manor house, where she is being lined up with her sisters for a family photograph, just before she is to meet young Edward.

A much more recent example of elegance in managing time comes in Seán O'Faoláin's story "Of Sanctity and Whiskey." Luke Regan, a successful portrait painter, is given a commission to come back to his old school, St. Killian's College, to paint a portrait of Brother Hilary, the retiring headmaster. He tries to recall Brother Hilary—but it has been forty years after all and, though he makes some quick sketches in his mind of the faculty he can remember ("He hoped he was not that old snob they used to call Dikey, a fellow with a face like a coffin and eyes like a dead hen's"), he can bring back nothing about his subject. The efforts to identify the man do, quite deftly and unobtrusively, take the story back to the wretched schoolboy days that (as we are beginning to learn) have marked for the worse all of Luke's later life.

When he meets Brother Hilary ("Nose rubicund, eyes blue as gentians, and an astonishingly protruding lower lip, the sure sign of a born talker"), he still cannot place him. The two become friendly. Then, as the painter concentrates on what he thinks will be a portrait of a benign old schoolmaster, the past begins to recreate itself in the sitter's face, and the Brother Hilary of forty years ago begins to appear in the painting:

Regan had his man whole and entire. The terror of his very first day at St. Killy's often repeated, seeing the lean black ghost come floating in. Like a starved wolf. One hand waving the leather strap behind his back like a black tail. The rasping voice. "What is a relative clause? Decline the verb see in the past tense. No, it is not! Hold out your hand. Take that. And that. And that." And always, the one thing all boys loathe in teachers, as sarcastic as acid.[4]

The portrait, of course, turns out to be Luke Regan's masterpiece—a masterpiece of such evil genius that his friends have to burn it while he is drunk.

Even in fiction that works complicated stratagems with time, there must, however, be some calendar of the present that goes from Monday to Tuesday and from 1986 to 1987. This is what we have called the "novelistic present" (though the actual tense may be either the present or the past). It is the line of continuity from which the time-shift departs and to which the time-shift must inevitably return, the main line of the story. The summonings of memory can have only one purpose—to illuminate and influence the present. They should never, either through garrulity or their own fascinations, overwhelm the intentions of the present story. If a writer suddenly finds that the part of the story he recovers from a former time is more interesting than what is supposed to be proceeding in the novelistic present, he must stop. He has begun too late; he has cast his story badly. He should make a new plan.

Another error is following an urge to recall the past in one long stretch, or several long stretches. Time present cannot stand motionless too long or it will have lost its momentum of interest for the reader; the sense of forward pace must be kept up. The best solution is to separate the past into several sequences and to work these into the present story separately and at appropriate places. There is no reason why, in the course of here-and-now, the past cannot be suggested, alluded to, or brought to attention without a formal journey into it. Dialogue is very useful for the purpose.

Another aspect of technique that interested the early twentieth-century fiction writers was the matter of tempo in the novel, the speed of its movement—from adagio through lento and andante to presto, one might say. Those experimenters Ford, Conrad, and James had confidence in a technique they borrowed partly from French writers and named the *progression d'effet*. As Ford explained it, that meant "every word set on paper must carry the story forward and . . . [it] must be carried forward faster and faster with more and more intensity." The trouble is that many good, or even great, novels will not fit the theory.

Another way of looking at this is shown in a wise remark of E. M. Forster's. He says that human beings lead two lives, "the life in time and the life by values." In other words (to change the metaphor), two clocks are running, the realistic chronometer and the eccentric clock of the emotions. "He waited for her no more than half an hour, but it seemed like forever" is a familiar example. Thirty minutes is real time, forever is value time. As mentioned earlier, narrative summary severely condenses real time, while the extended scene runs on value time. And nothing differs more drastically among individual authors than their concepts of value time. One novelist finds that it takes a long chapter for his heroine, like Violetta in *La Traviata,* to collapse and die. He prolongs the scene, wringing every drop of emotion from it.

Another novelist, having prepared us for the sad event,

might do it starkly, briefly, and with understatement. The first writer says, "The agony of parting seemed to stretch on endlessly." The second says, "It happened so quickly we had no time to say good-bye." (Only the doctor noted that death occurred exactly thirty-seven minutes after the first hemorrhage; but he did not write a novel.)

Thus, at the very beginning of a work of fiction (unless it is to be something experimental), the writer should be prepared to record actual time so that the work makes sense; but, beyond that, he should be prepared to make his stresses, his large meanings, his high drama occur in value time. And, to do that, he must know his values.

MATTERS OF TENSE

The simple past tense has always been the favored vehicle of English narrative from Chaucer on through most of the twentieth century. There was occasional necessity for the perfect or the past perfect in recalling facts or events from an earlier time, and the present tense was sometimes called up. The present, of course, is an essential for dialogue, and some of the nineteenth-century novelists found it a good addition for a change of pace or for special effects. Possibly the most extensive—and most virtuosic—use of the present appears in *Bleak House.* There Dickens alternated between the simple past in "Esther's Story" and a present-tense narrative in the rest of the book. Here is a sample; the lawyer, Mr. Tulkinghorn, pays a visit to the garret room of the mysterious copyist of legal documents:

On a low bed opposite the fire, a confusion of dirty patchwork, lean-ribbed ticking, and coarse sacking, the lawyer, hesitating just within the doorway, sees a man. He lies there, dressed in shirt and trousers, with bare feet. He has a yellow look in the spectral darkness of a candle that has guttered down, until the whole length of its wick (still burning) has doubled over and left a tower of winding sheet above it. His hair is ragged, mingling with his whiskers and his beard—the latter, ragged too, and grown, like the scum and mist around him, in neglect.[5]

What was a novelty for Dickens and his contemporaries became, in the early 1960s, almost a standard usage by young American fiction writers. John Updike's *Rabbit Run* (1960) was an influential example. It was not long before practically all stories in the literary magazines and most novels by writers under forty were told in the present tense. It became the most frequent cliché of technique in the new fiction.

The reasons are not at all obscure. The present tense gives a striking sense of "nowness," of immediacy, to the story. Writers have always hoped to make the reader see it happening before his eyes and the past tense gives a little distance, or a little temporal remoteness, to the story. To the writers of the past twenty years or so, the present tense seemed to have more energy, more of a confrontational quality than the simple past. It is more exciting and faster-moving.

But, like any device of technique, it has both uses and abuses. By its very briskness, it tends to disguise an author's essential lack of personal style. No one could read a present-tense passage in *Bleak House* without perceiving the hand of a master stylist. On the other hand, one might read passages from Bobbie Ann Mason, Raymond Carver, Ann Beattie, and a supermarket ad without distinguishing an individual author. (This is not to deny that the first three are gifted writers with admirable books to their credit. They simply do not wish to be stylists in the traditional sense.)

Another negative aspect of the present-tense usage is its sheer ubiquity. No one seems to be going very fast when every car on the highway is traveling at seventy. No facade seems very striking when each house on the block is freshly painted the same color. No time is relative with others when everything is happening this very instant. The best fiction, finally, should not be an affair of the moment. It should have long memories and portents about the future.

Notes to Chapter 7

1. From *Distortions* (Garden City, N.Y.: Doubleday & Co., 1976), pp. 223–24.

2. From the collection *The Ballad of the Sad Café* (Boston: Houghton Mifflin Co., 1951), p. 41.

3. New York: Alfred A. Knopf, 1951; pp. 134–35.

4. From *The Collected Stories of Seán O'Fáolain* (Boston: Little, Brown & Co., 1983), p. 1042.

5. New York: Heritage Press, 1942; p. 142.

EIGHT

PLOT AND STORY

The invention of the campfire and the invention of the story
in prehistoric times probably came close together, and the
earliest titles may have been something like, "How Og Killed
a Bear," or "How We Stole the Fruit from the Other Cave."
Along with these reports of experience, there must have been
stories of dreams, memorials for dead heroes, tall-tale lies,
and comic squibs. As E. M. Forster describes it in his *Aspects
of the Novel,* story is the most ancient and fundamental way
of arranging any narration of events. Plot, he notes, is an
invention of a later date for more sophisticated listeners. The
ancestor of plot was a set religious ritual, and out of that came
the drama, the first kind of story with a scheme of action and
reaction.

Fiction learned from drama and plot became one of the
great facts of life in the short story and novel from mediaeval
fabliaux (popular French tales of the thirteenth and four-
teenth centuries) on through the twentieth century. Some
writers have accepted it cheerfully as a convention, others

have found it a fine discipline, and still others have regarded it as a tyranny. Here are some varied opinions:

As regards plots I find real life no help at all. Real life seems to have no plots. [Ivy Compton-Burnett]

Plots are indeed what the story-writer sees with, and so do we as we read. The plot is the Why. Why? is asked and replied to at various depths; the fishes in the sea are bigger the deeper we go. [Eudora Welty]

Plot must further the novel toward its object. Plot is the knowing of destination. [Elizabeth Bowen]

The author always loads his dice, but he must never let the reader see that he has done so, and by the manipulation of his plot, he can engage the reader's attention so that he does not perceive what violence has been done to him. [Somerset Maugham]

What I think is more important in the short story is the plot or situation, while in the novel what's important are the characters. . . . In writing a novel, you should know all about the characters and any plot will do, while in a short story it is the situation that counts. [Jorge Luis Borges]

The plot, since it is the imitation of an action, must confine itself to one complete action alone. The structure of the parts must be so interrelated that, if any one of them is moved or taken away, the whole plot will be distorted. [Aristotle]

Each of these commentators is noting, from a different angle, the principal thing that distinguishes fiction from the artless chronicle of events. Thus, plot is an artifice. It arouses and directs the reader's expectations. It has the sense of predestination. It imposes a unity on the narration so that the happenings must connect, in the end, to make a whole. The application of this kind of strategy is what has made the art of modern fiction possible.

Forster makes a very clear and useful distinction between story and plot, saying first that story is a simple arrangement of events in their sequence. For example: "The king died and then the queen died." Plot, on the other hand, is that same time sequence with the addition of causality: "The king died and then the queen died of grief." Then, to strengthen the plot with a little suspense: "The queen died, no one knew why, until it was discovered that it was through grief at the death of the king." Forster comments that the question put to the story is always "And then?" but the question asked of the plot is always "Why?"

To differentiate them still further: the story is the road of time, proceeding from the known to the unknown and meeting each event in succession. A plot, on the other hand, is a pattern of cause and effect that is always in process of change. One event causes another to occur or a happening causes something unknown until now to be revealed. The basis of a plot is the combining of situation and characters—characters acting in their individual ways within some set of circumstances. The dynamic part of plot is the progressive change and development of that situation. It is only at the end, when the events have reached culmination, that the pattern is complete.

This is the place for a word of caution. The terms "plot" and "story" are here used as E. M. Forster defines them in *Aspects of the Novel*. Other authors have frequently regarded them as interchangeable or have blurred the difference between the two. Forster's useful distinction will be used in this chapter but, elsewhere in the book, the word "story" has the more general sense of any coherent recital of events in fiction.

Forster considers story the more primitive form because it depends on curiosity alone as to what happens next. In contrast, the ability to grasp a plot requires both memory and intelligence. The constant suggestion of "Why?" in a plot poses mystery and, he says, "To appreciate a mystery, part of the mind must be left behind, brooding, while the other part goes marching on." Finally, Forster notes, the result of a successful plot is "something aesthetically compact . . . beauty at which a novelist should never aim, though he fails if he does not achieve it."

The idea of plot entered into fiction slowly and hesitantly. Despite Aristotle's adequate critical definition and the long tradition of plot in drama, fiction remained a matter of story throughout its early history. French *fabliaux* and Italian *novelle* (*novelle* are the Italian popular tales of the thirteenth to sixteenth centuries) had elementary plots, usually on the theme of illicit-love-unmasked or illicit-love-rewarded. *Don Quixote* is an example of the story-novel, primitive by Forster's definition but with strong characters and a mighty, satirical purpose. Defoe and Smollett followed in the line. But, with the work of their contemporaries Fielding and Richardson, novels began to take on a plot formation, and that is why they are often called the first novelists in English. In the nineteenth century, novelists at last mastered plot and, delighted with the literary equivalent of the steam engine, discovered virtuoso ways of using it, frequently to the point of foolish ingenuity. The classic mystery story with its puzzle plot and the surprise-ending story are examples of some of these uses.

The reaction set in with the splendid Russian fiction writers of the late nineteenth century, who used plot but were seldom bound by it. The English-writing world noticed and was impressed. In the early twentieth century, Chekhov's style of short story began to look better than Maupassant's, and Tolstoy loomed larger than Dickens or Balzac in the novel. The tendency to minimize plot in favor of other values can be seen early in the stories of Sherwood Anderson, Katherine Mansfield, and Ernest Hemingway and in such novelists as Virginia Woolf and James Joyce.

THE CLASSIC PLOT

To go back to the origins—Aristotle in his *Poetics* gave the classic definition of plot and laid out the principles that have affected the practice of writers ever since. But Aristotle's chief point of reference was Greek tragedy. Quite a few of his formulations have been much debated and much modified, but they still have relevance to the craft of fiction.

The important thing is shape. Aristotle saw plot as an action complete and whole, one with a beginning, a middle, and an end. The end must be some kind of logical outcome or culmination of the events in the beginning and middle. That action arises from one of the natural situations of human life. As the logic of probability or necessity brings new events, that situation is changed. And all of these events are aimed at a single (and, in terms of the plot), inevitable outcome. Along with this goes the idea of the three unities—of action, time, and place (Aristotle himself demanded the first one only; neoclassical critics of the sixteenth century developed the idea of the other two). The time covered by the drama, the area of its physical setting, and the scope of its action all ought to be limited to a small compass. That meant that the action must concern itself with one problem, take place within twenty-four hours, and confine itself to one place or one city.

These strict unities, however, proved to be too binding for Shakespeare and his fellow dramatists and they are, of course, too narrow for most fiction. Classical tragedy required a burning concentration to create its pity, terror, and the final purging of the emotions. It is too fierce and exclusive a discipline for fiction, which always wants to take in far more of the great mixed bag of life's experience.

Aristotle distinguished two kinds of plot—the "simple" plot, which closely resembles Forster's "story," and the "complex" plot. To see how these work, here is a standard working model of the Aristotelian mechanism:

At the beginning is the establishment of the situation. Characters are defined; they are placed in some kind of relationship (allied, opposed, or simply observational). The situation is in progress; that is, one or more of the characters has strong intentions. He, or they, want something very clearly. These wants or intentions are usually of the most straightforward kind—a young woman looks forward to her marriage, or a young man leaves the poverty of home to make his fortune in the city, and so on.

The next stage of the plot has been called the "rising action." The situation develops along the lines hinted at in the beginning and the characters pursue their intentions, not without opposition but with apparent success. This "rising action" leads to the first great turning point of the plot, which Aristotle called the "reversal of the situation." Along comes an event that seems to lead to quite a normal turn of the story we have been following—but, instead, it suddenly puts a new (and sometimes disastrous) face on the situation. As an example, Aristotle cites the arrival of the messenger who has come to relieve Oedipus's fears about his mother the queen, but who ends up by revealing the king's true identity, thus forcing a complete reappraisal of the circumstances.

This reappraisal, which is the second turning point, follows swiftly and inevitably. Aristotle calls it the "recognition." It is the moment when characters become aware of the drastic change that has been made in their relationships. The "reversal" alters the world they live in by introducing hitherto-unknown facts; the revolution of facts then produces a revolution of ideas and emotions, which is "recognition."

The trouble with these definitions, however, is that they were designed to fit the tragic drama Aristotle was discussing. Instead of the word "reversal," a broader and better term for understanding fiction would be the term "crisis." Aristotle's "reversal" depends on a thunderbolt of fate. It is true that the men of tragedy have unwittingly demanded it and have made themselves targets for it, but it still arrives from the skies. A fictional crisis, on the other hand, is earth-born and human. It comes from the opposite forces put in motion during the "rising action" of the story. It is very likely that the wants or intentions of the characters will collide here.

(Aristotle felt that he was describing a kind of drama that was consistent and logical. He speaks of it as following "the law of probability or necessity," and wants only the development that is "inevitable." Yet that drama is heavily and obviously dependent on a chain of coincidence—the sudden revelation of secret information in the "reversal" scene being a prime example. In another place, he mentions "the statue of Mitys at Argos, which fell upon his murderer and killed him." Aristotle goes on to observe that "such events seem not to be due to mere chance.")

For Aristotle, the "reversal" is the past, like a time bomb, taking revenge on the present. However limited his theory was, it does lead to the more inclusive idea of crisis and it does make that invaluable point about "recognition." The crisis should force a psychological transformation—one or more of the characters has to accept an entirely new view of the world around him. The old pattern of human relationships is broken up and another has to take its place.

The classical formula names the next step the "falling action," the postclimax events that lead toward the final resolution. In classical tragedy, that final scene is called the "catastrophe," an ending in deep sorrow, destruction, or death. In comedy and in the peculiarly mixed form called fiction, the resolution scene is called the "denouement" (which comes from a French verb meaning to unknot). It is the point where everything comes clear. A more innocent age saw it as the grand moment when disguises were cast off, mistaken identities revealed, long-lost relatives reunited, parted lovers joined, mysteries solved, and villains given just deserts. When the early playwright or storyteller was at a loss to put everything right, he would send out for what the Romans called a "deus ex machina"—a god from the machine (lowered, quite literally, onto the stage by mechanism in some dramas), who would quickly solve all pending problems. In more modern drama, he took the form of a rich uncle or benefactor who forgives Clifford, reunites him with Sophronia, and provides a liberal cash settlement.

This simplified drawing of the plot structure does not take into consideration the many elaborations or variations possible—such things as double plots, the use of mystery, surprise endings, and so on. Nor does it suggest how the invention can be used for better or for worse, how it can give form and strength to fiction, or how it can give a false and artificial impression. Here are some actual practices and some writers' opinions.

ONE EXAMPLE OF THE CLASSIC PLOT

This example is furnished by a very unpretentious story ("The Clown") from Alberto Moravia's *Roman Tales*. It is told by a man who goes from restaurant to restaurant playing his guitar. The other half of his act is a clownish singer named Milone. The story follows the classical plot structure so unobtrusively that the reader is hardly aware of the method:

Establishment   The narrator describes Milone, a heavy, awkward man with no singing talent but some small gift for parody. He tends to overdo everything, especially his broad burlesque of women singers. The narrator finds this kind of clowning indecent and despises Milone, but he sticks with him because the act is popular and brings in a good income.

Rising action   He goes on to describe a typical scene in a middle-class restaurant where Milone is doing something vulgar with a simple popular ballad. The audience enjoys it; far from being offended, the ladies are enthusiastic. Later, Milone gets the idea of dressing up in women's clothes and wants his accompanist to do likewise. The narrator is disgusted. "Isn't it about time you invented something attractive, something moving?" he asks. "People want to laugh," says Milone, "and I make them laugh."

Crisis   One day, the two entertainers happen into a poor wine bar, and Milone, for no reason except vanity, decides to sing. As usual, he distorts and destroys a beautiful song. But, after he finishes, a handsome young man in workman's overalls steps up and says furiously, "Now I'll sing it for you." And he does, making the song beautiful again. The onlookers are indifferent, but, when the young man goes back to his table, the girl who has been waiting for him throws her arms around him. Milone and the narrator know why he has sung the song.

Recognition   All that the narrator ever sees is a "bitter expression" on Milone's face. He has to suppose—and to supply for us—what must have gone on in the clown's mind after the blow:

I have said that Milone's head had been turned, and that he believed himself to be a great artist of some kind whereas in reality he was just a poor wretch who played the buffoon to amuse people while they were eating; so much the greater, therefore, was the downfall brought about by that fair-haired young man in overalls. I think that, while the young man was singing, he must have seen himself, all of a sudden, not as he had hitherto believed himself to be, but as he really was—a clumsy, big man of fifty who put on a bib and recited nursery rhymes. But I also think that he must have realized that he would never be able to sing, even if he made a pact with the devil. All he could do, in fact, was to make people laugh; and the only way he could make them laugh was by holding certain things up to ridicule. And those things, it so happened, were just the things he had never succeeded in having in his own life.[1]

Catastrophe The next morning it is discovered that Milone has hanged himself in his room. The narrator is the only one who goes along to see him buried. He notes an appropriately grotesque touch—the landlady sells the rope, piece by piece, for souvenirs.

This is no more than a thumbnail tragedy, but it is almost a success because the author is sure of most of his moves. He does not describe the narrator's love affair; he doesn't describe how Milone spends his money or how he was brought up. He quietly bases his story on the traditional scheme of the plot, adapting here and there as necessary.

Beyond that, the story gets its strength from exactly the same source as tragedy. Only a man who is capable of feeling is capable of such disastrous self-recognition. The narrator, and thus the reader, are led to misjudge Milone in the first part of the story and to think that he is incapable of any shame. But his hidden flaw turns out to be his very ability to think, feel, and to apply a moral judgment to himself. Paradoxically, the death of the unknown Milone becomes a small tragedy.

One critical objection that has been raised about this

story is to the effect that Milone is first presented as one type
of man and then, through the action of the story, a surprise
occurs and he is shown to be another type. The narrator and
reader have watched an unexpected transformation. But is the
transformation, indeed, so unexpected? Sometimes people
seem most antagonistic to those things they secretly wish they
could have or attain—it is the reaction of bitter frustration.
There are two things that Milone burlesques brutally—beautiful song and women. They are "just the things he never
succeeded in having in his own life." (As far as anyone
knows, Milone has never had a wife or girlfriend, and he is
definitely a very bad singer, though he has tried to learn all
the popular songs.) At one point, the narrator speaks to him
about "the passion [he puts into] jeering at them." From
these strong hints, we get an idea of what Milone has once
longed for and been denied. When the young workman sings
a song beautifully and is embraced by his girl, the moment
sums up Milone's lifelong failure—and it is probably then
that he decides to kill himself.

Now there is one very awkward aspect to the plotting of
this story. Moravia reached the recognition scene and found
that he could do it by supposition only. The reason is that he
has left all of the telling to the narrator and has made Milone
remain almost silent. It would be a mistake in characterization to have him become articulate after the scene in the wine
bar and to express the self-revulsion he must have been
feeling. In the quoted passage, therefore, the narrator must
guess the whole of the recognition. He guesses shrewdly, and
no doubt accurately, but there is no hiding the fact that the
most important character exits without leaving a single clue

except for that "bitter expression." The author (disguised as the narrator) is sitting there summarizing what must or what might have happened in Milone's heart. As dramatists know, the recognition has to take place within our view. Watching and listening to a man as his world falls apart before his eyes is a shocking thing. But it is the essential shock of tragedy —even this minor one.

A PLOT IN SEARCH OF AN ENDING

In his *A Writer's Notebook*, Somerset Maugham relates an incident somebody once told him and says that he has been unable to use it for a story. The anecdote goes this way:

Two young Englishmen were working on a tea plantation in the hills of India. One of them—call him A—always got ten or twelve letters in every mail, but B, his colleague never got any. B was envious. One day, he pointed out the disparity and said to his friend, "I'll give you five pounds for one of your letters." A agreed and spread out his newly arrived and unopened letters on the table, saying "Take your choice." After dinner, A casually asked, "By the way, what was that letter about?" B refused to tell. "Who was it from?" A asked. B said that was his own business. There was a brief quarrel, but B would not budge.

Then, after a week of worry and imagining things, A went to B and offered to buy the letter back. "Not on your life," B said. "It's my letter and I won't give it up."

Maugham comments: "I suppose that if I belonged to the modern school of story writers, I should write it just as it is and leave it. It goes against the grain with me. I want a story

to have form, and I don't see how you can give it that unless
you can bring it to a conclusion that leaves no legitimate room
for questioning. But even if you could bring yourself to leave
the reader up in the air, you don't want to leave yourself up
in the air with him."[2]

What are some of the possible endings? First, we should
note that Maugham is saying that the story demands an ending that will tell the reader what was in the letter and what
happened as a result—so that no one will be left "up in the
air." With that, it is not too difficult to think of some Maugham-
esque possibilities:

1. B relents and agrees to give the letter back if A will give
   him two letters from the next mail. That mail being a
   month away, A agrees. When A reads the letter, he finds
   it of no consequence. But, when a month later B gets two
   letters from the batch, A begins to worry again. The process is repeated until B is getting—and answering—all of
   A's mail. He effectively controls A's communication with
   the outside world, and A begins to think that murder is the
   only solution.
2. A month goes by and B suddenly announces that he is
   leaving. A is left behind in charge of the tea plantation,
   but it is a routine job with no hope of promotion. Some
   years later, on a trip to Calcutta, he meets an official of the
   company that owns (among many others) the tea plantation. The official tells him that B has prospered and is now
   in charge of all the company's interests in Ceylon—he's
   now a rich and important man. And, the official adds, "We
   never quite understood why you neglected to reply to the
   letter in which we offered you the promotion. As you know,

if we didn't hear from you within a month, B would be offered the position—and he seems to have done very well from it."

There are, in any case, numbers of possible endings that would bring the story down to earth in Maugham's way. But are those stories worth writing? They seem to leave the personal element quite out of the equation—we have no idea of the individuality of the two men who face each other day after day in that lonely bungalow in the hills. Once we have given them real personalities, however, those personalities begin to control what happens in the story. And once A and B have become, say, Andrew and Brian, believable characters, it will be very hard to confine the story to an anecdote with a punch-line ending. The little incident of the purchased letter and A's attempt to get it back would then become just the opening situation to lead into a longer and richer story about, say, a complicated relationship between two young men far from home.

PRACTICAL SUGGESTIONS ABOUT PLOT

In early stories or a first novel, the writer is usually prudent to follow traditional lines of construction. Having learned the fundamentals of his craft, he can then go on confidently to departures or experiments. On the other hand, the plot outline below is not to be taken as a beginner's straitjacket—he can adapt it freely to the purposes of his story as long as he does not abandon the principles noted and the idea of consistent development.

Introduction of oppositions   In establishing the primary situation of his story, the writer should create opposing forces or contending ideas for the sake of tension. More specific words for this are: conflict, doubt, problem, struggle, rivalry. It may be a matter of conflict within the mind of one person or it may be external conflict. The important thing is to show the reader that there is a pressure to decide between or among alternatives.

Deepening of the oppositions   If the opposing forces stay in balance or if they are inactive, there will never be a story. Once they are established, they must grow graver, heading toward a flash point. This is the developmental part of the plot and here the tensions steadily increase.

The flash point or crisis   The opposing forces are now fully realized and fully focused, and they must reach a crisis. They can no longer coexist in the story.

The resolution   After the crisis is over, the world of the fiction has changed for better or for worse. Perhaps the characters we identify with have been blessed with success, or half success. Perhaps they have been deceived by an apparent success, although we know better. Or perhaps they have failed to gain a small objective but have won in a larger sense. These are just a few of the many possibilities the resolution may bring about.

CHANCE AND COINCIDENCE

"Real life seems to have no plot." When fiction turned from the story's natural "and then, and then" to drama's "then, because," it gave up a certain honesty about life. The problem of fitting believable events to a dramatic pattern held little fear for the Greek dramatists, who knew that their audiences accepted the idea of fate as quite real. But for the fiction writer, who does not have the fates or the gods at his disposal, there are dangerous risks.

Any writer of more or less realistic fiction depends very heavily on his credibility; he is trying to persuade the reader that his story-vision has verisimilitude to life in the observed world. So, whenever his fictional events seem to be manipulated for the sake of plot alone, he is in trouble with the ordinary skepticism of his reader. We believe in cause and effect in human relationships, but only when they seem justified by experience. For one example of a wise negative, here is a quotation from a 1973 memo from the *Atlantic Monthly* to its readers: "Subject: Stories we do not want to read or edit: Those that ask the reader to blame society for misfortunes inflicted on the characters by the author."

Sheer chance or coincidence has always been the bad magic of the plot. The god from the machine delivered happy endings but he destroyed all credulity at the same time. In present-day writing, one mark of commercial or second-rate fiction is the obvious use of coincidence. It is easy to forget the many good writers who, struggling with the stubborn material of the plot, have given in to temptation, or how seductive coincidence can be to an inexperienced writer.

On the other hand, we all believe in chance and coincidence. "Truth is stranger than fiction," people are fond of remarking, yet seldom does anybody say, "Fiction is stranger than truth." Tricks of chance that happen often in real life would be scorned if they appeared in a story. The answer to the paradox is that there are perfectly natural kinds of chance and quite acceptable coincidences. It is by chance, of course, that Anna Karenina meets, of all the cavalry officers in the Russian army, just the man called Vronsky. But, because she has an affinity for that kind of man, we accept the notion without question. If we can say of this or that character in fiction, "She would have sacrificed her life in caring for somebody else whether her invalid husband had lived or not," or "He would have succeeded in getting rich no matter where or when he lived," chance is nicely balanced with causality to make a convincing fiction.

One of the oldest and wisest remarks ever made about literature or life is Heraclitus's observation that "character is destiny." It should be written on the wall of every novelist's study. It is, however, only half the dynamics of plot. The given situation is the other half. Human character—desires, weaknesses, virtues, aberrations, etc.—creates actions within situations. That is, in the beginning of any fiction, we have a certain set of circumstances and a singular human character. The character deals with the circumstances in his characteristic way, and thus the story moves into a changed situation, and another, and at last to an outcome we can accept as the character's fitting destiny.

It is when the writer deserts the kind of fate that flows from character and substitutes something that comes from a cast of the dice that he is cheating. There is, of course, that perfectly wild, unpredictable, fortuituous happening of the kind everybody has noticed at least once. The odds are ten million to one against its ever occurring, yet there it is. There is no reason why an author shouldn't use a coincidence of the kind in his fiction, but, if he uses it to keep his plot wheels turning or to make things turn out in the end, beware.

Mark Twain, in his famous essay on James Fenimore Cooper's literary offenses, said, "The personages of a tale shall confine themselves to possibilities and let miracles alone; or, if they venture a miracle, the author must so plausibly set it forth as to make it look possible and reasonable." This, as it should be, is not so much a plea for strictly naturalistic fiction as it is a plea for fair play on the part of the author. Literature offers quite a few examples of unscrupulous plot miracles set down on the page by the good and even the great.

Shakespeare's worst offense against the law is *Othello*. In that play, he constructed his plot out of the most incredible patchwork of chance—a lost handkerchief taken as a clue, an overheard conversation that is misunderstood, characters failing to say the obvious thing at the right time and instead saying the obviously wrong thing. What saves the play from disaster is the fact that Shakespeare had the right thing working as well—and no reader or watcher can escape the sense that Othello's character is his destiny, that noble gullibility can cause more woe than distrustful meanness.

Dickens, of course, is the greatest inventor of fantastic coincidence in the whole of English literature. His plots grow and thrive on the purely fortuitous—but so openly and systematically that they seem to be a special case. He uses coincidence not simply with a stroke here and there to rationalize or explain something but almost as a universal connective by which one character or group of characters has its interests involved with others'.

Thomas Hardy raised the idea of chance (or, as he called it, "hap") to a supernatural principle something like a combination of the Greek Nemesis and the three Fates. His plots frequently turn on what seems to be random luck, yet his purpose is not the conventional one of creating a surprise, rescuing a character from a dilemma, or making a happy ending possible. Hardy thought that hap was the perverse, blind, and wanton force that brought human intentions to nothing, and he made it appear at crucial moments to upset lives and bring down disaster.

There is a curious example of another kind of coincidence in Stendhal's great novel *The Red and the Black*, and this is a matter of forecasting a future event precisely rather than of hooking the plot together. The hero, Julien Sorel, as a young man, sets out to be interviewed for a job as tutor to the mayor's children. On his way, he stops at a village church and sits down in the pew belonging to the mayor's family. There he finds a slip of newspaper that says, "Details of the execution and of the last moments of Louis Jenrel, executed at Besançon, on the. . . ." On the other side of the paper are the words "The first step." On his way out, he thinks he sees blood near the holy water stoup, but it is only a red reflection. He has an obscure fright, but then says to himself, "Should I prove coward? *To arms!*"

Oddly enough, this is no vague omen but a set of exact clues about events still far in the future. Louis Jenrel is both a rhyme and an anagram for Julien Sorel. Julien, with his tutor's job, is about to take the first step toward his crime. It is in this very pew that he will shoot Madame de Rênal and her blood will fall on this floor. *"To arms!"* suggests the literal pistol. Finally, Julien will be executed at Besançon.

Looking back from the end of the book, the reader remembers this little prophecy as a startling mistake. Stendhal's superb development of his hero's psychology throughout the story has persuaded us that Julien's rise and then his sudden self-destruction are the destiny created by character. But can we be so sure? That little slip of paper in the church pew seems to be a sign of some highly contrived predestination.

"It so happened that . . ."; "Now by chance it occurred . . ."; "Quite unexpectedly she found herself. . . ."—these and their equivalents are danger signs for the fiction writer. Some plot requirement is about to win at the expense of naturalness.

Fortunately, most modern writers of serious fiction have learned to avoid the clumsy artifices of chance and coincidence and the Victorian plot-props have largely disappeared. It is chiefly in the subgenres of fiction—science fiction, mysteries, suspense stories, romances, and best-seller fiction that these tricks live on.

PREVIEWS OF EVENTS TO COME

Stendhal's forecast of Julien's fate suggests a note on another device once favored by novelists but nowadays seldom seen in serious work. It is the trick of borrowing some piece of information from the still-unknown future of the story or novel in order to add a hint of anticipation to the present event. It is called the "had I but known" method, and its trademarks are such introductions as, "Had I but known what

danger awaited me, I never would have opened that door";
or "Little did Catherine realize that she was about to meet
someone who would change her life"; or "Looking back on
it later, I knew that I should have taken warning from these
words."

Occasionally, a fatuous preview is put in not to arouse
suspense but to dispel it. In *Barchester Towers*, Trollope—a
man ever mindful of sensitive nerves—remarks: "But let the
gentle-hearted reader be under no apprehension whatsoever.
It is not destined that Eleanor shall marry Mr. Slope or Bertie
Stanhope."

There are two questions of technique here—the question
of the intrusive author, which has been discussed in an earlier
chapter, and the question of orderly plot development. It is
wrong to remind the reader of "the violence that is being done
to him." If there is one illusion that must be fostered, it is
the reader's sense that he sits observing the process of people
working out certain problems of life on their own terms.
When the author casts ahead for a moment, he gives the show
away. He admits that those problems of life are his own
tawdry invention and that all is predetermined.

Graham Greene nearly succeeds in spoiling a fine short
story, "The Basement Room," with an anachronism of this
kind. He wants to tell us that his small boy protagonist is
going through a traumatic experience that will blight his life
to come, and so Greene keeps stepping in to inform us that
"he would never escape that scene. In a week, he had forgotten it, but it would condition his career, the long austerity of
his life." That observation has no connection with the plot
because the story does not deal with the rest of the boy's life,

but those sententious bits of popular psychology do tend to weaken the reader's interest in the present story.

Quite distinct from this kind of ruse, there is a perfectly legitimate way of anticipating the future. One of the indispensable ingredients in fiction is the promise of something. It is the sort of low common denominator of all readable books. In the best fiction, the promises are put with subtlety —it may be simply that we have seen a certain trait of character in A and we anticipate the moment when she is going to resoundingly encounter B, who is just her opposite. It may be that we realize that C is pathologically stingy and, when we see him getting into a situation that is going to demand some heavy spending, we anticipate certain consequences. Anything, in short, that is presented to the reader as interestingly incomplete anticipates the future.

THE DEVICE OF MYSTERY

Withholding certain information until it can be revealed most effectively has always been an important part of plot construction. Every plot has an element of mystery in it that raises the question *why* about people and their actions, but (excluding the pure mystery or detective story, which has its own conventions) the way that question is raised and later answered is all-important. The tactics to avoid are these:

1. It is a mistake to confide in the reader through one character's point of view while withholding something that character knows.

2. It is a mistake to conceal something merely for the sake of mystification.
3. It is a mistake to sensationalize any mystery with portentous trappings or actions that have nothing to do with the main enigma.
4. It is a mistake to introduce gratuitous mystery that contributes nothing to the unfolding of plot or character.

These tactics strike the intelligent reader as cheap and underhanded. One of the ways to steer clear of them is for the writer to keep a clear sense of what the reader knows at any point in the story as compared to what the main character or characters know. It is perfectly legitimate to permit the reader to be ahead of the character who is acting as the point of view. This is true of almost every story using the point of view of a child, an adult of limited intelligence, or any person who is excluded from a full understanding of events. In these cases, the reader comprehends in a "superior" way what is going on and what is likely to happen. An example of this is the last-cited Graham Greene story. The boy Philip sees his friend Baines, the butler, who is married to the terrible-tempered Mrs. Baines, having a rendezvous with a pretty young woman. At first, it does not enter Philip's head to be suspicious, but it does ours.

The counterpart mistake is to have a set of facts clearly before the eyes of the characters without their making the obvious deductions. If Philip, as a young man, had failed to guess what Baines was up to, we must conclude that there is something wrong either with his intelligence or the author's.

On the other hand, the narrator or point of view must never be ahead of the reader. Esther Summerson is the narrator in part of Dickens's *Bleak House;* she confides in the reader about most things she knows but hides others for the sake of the plot, and we feel tricked. For another example, if John searches Sidney's desk and finds the telltale letter, the author is honor-bound to give us the contents.

Most modern writers who use some strand of mystery in their stories prefer to lay the emphasis on *how,* not *who.* That is, they interest the reader in motivations—how, for example, Mr. A has behaved in the past so that he now hasn't a friend in the world. Or, we may know that B and C—both good people—are deadly enemies and we want to know what first made them clash. The mystery of *who,* in contrast, belongs to the classic detective story. It is an effort to identify the responsible—usually the guilty—person. Who committed the murders in the Rue Morgue? Who killed Roger Ackroyd? Variants of that mystery are: Where is the missing will concealed? What is behind that bricked-up wall in the cellar?

When a writer centers interest on the discovery of such facts, he is concentrating on a logical puzzle. When, writing more serious fiction, he centers his mystery on motivation, on the desires and beliefs of his people, he generally makes the "mystery" contribute to the mainstream of his story. The solution to a factual mystery is often a letdown because the suspense promises more bang than the solution can deliver. A well-done solution of a motivational mystery can add to the library of humane letters.

THE TWIST AT THE END

The surprise ending, or the reversal of the situation at the close of a short story, was a favorite device of Maupassant and was popularized in American fiction by O. Henry. It proves the ingenuity of the author. It tells us once again that life is full of ironies—those diamonds the woman worked all her life to pay for are discovered to have been paste. It is a long version of the anecdote or joke, and its use is now confined to the mystery novel (where, as a trick among tricks, it is perfectly legitimate) and television dramas.

THE DOUBLE PLOT, THE SUBPLOT, AND THE MULTIPLE PLOT

A great many novels and a few short stories carry forward two or more plots at the same time. In English literature, the tradition comes from a favorite convention of the Elizabethan drama. The general rule of sixteenth- and seventeenth-century plays was to develop a main plot whose highborn characters were the ones with whom the audience identified and sympathized. The subplot was carried out by characters from the lower orders, and it was usually comic. The two plots were often different sides of the same drama, and the subplot could be a joking comment on the main action or an ironic mirror. The tribulations of love between the aristocratic lovers are reflected in the comic mishaps of love between two of their servants. The denouement would finally resolve both plots.

The attraction of this parallel construction was the playwright's chance to exploit an idea from two different angles. There could be a serious comparison as well as a comic contrast. *King Lear* is a good example of that with its two different views of children-parent relationships. Whatever its purpose might be, the double plot gave the onlooker a sense of moving about freely in the world of the play, of knowing what the duke was like and also knowing what his servants and soldiers thought of him. It was the beginning of the tendency to expand and explore that would later give so much energy to the nineteenth-century novel.

The general purposes of the double plot are much the same in fiction as in the drama, but novelists have discovered new variations. One of the most daring experiments in the form is *Wuthering Heights.* The traditional method of working the two plots is to keep them roughly parallel in chronology and to alternate the narrative between them. Emily Brontë's striking conception is to tell, in effect, the same story twice, once with a tragic ending and once with a happy outcome. Rather than alternating, one follows the other. The main plot is that of Heathcliff, Catherine, and Edgar. This leads to the subplot enacted by the children, young Cathy, Linton, and Hareton. In the second generation, roles correspond to those of the first, but the characters within the roles have altered —the romantic violence of Heathcliff and Catherine has burned itself out. This becomes more than a double-plot device because Brontë answers her question twice with opposite visions of what might have happened.

Jane Austen's *Pride and Prejudice* has a totally different use of the double plot. Here the plots are so closely alike in substance that it is only the small reversal of events from one to the other (Bingley is prevailed upon to reject Jane; Elizabeth then rejects Darcy) and shadings of character that separate the two. It is like watching two slightly different aspects of the same experience and thus concentrating our attention on one subject. (There is, of course, the second subplot of

Lydia and Wickham, a contrasting one that shows the dangers of making love a game rather than a serious business of the moral nature and the intellect.) Jane Austen's kind of fiction was intensive. She was more interested in varieties of the same experience than in many contrasting experiences.

With Dickens, the multiplicity of plot almost reached the stage of anarchy. That tendency of the drama to reach out for wider experience expands into an effort to organize multitudes of people and greatly differing areas of society into many interlocking stories. Sometimes it is like a ten-ring circus with a lion coming into the pony act, a pony on the tightrope, and the acrobats getting involved with the clowns. As Frank O'Connor remarks about Dickens's *Dombey and Son:*

> . . . we get a straightforward picture of a hard-hearted, arrogant business man who pays no attention to his little daughter, Florence, and whose life is bound up with his son, Paul, who, he hopes, will succeed him in the business. But Paul's mother has died, so he acquires a wet-nurse, Mrs. Toodle, who in turn fans out into a number of entertaining characters; while in a sub-plot, the hero, Walter, who loves Florence, is the nephew of a wonderful old character called Solomon Gills, and Solomon has as friend an equally wonderful character, Captain Cuttle, who, in turn has a friend . . .[3]

It often happens that Dickens's energy and imagination seem to turn away from his pale, conventional hero and heroine and their plot, toward the comic or melodramatic possibilities in other lives. Thus, the center does not hold. The reliable rule of the drama was to assume that we are all a part of the same life and that the same human motives only work themselves out somewhat differently on different levels. Dickens's fantastic imagination did not permit him to believe this. His multiple worlds do not reflect but exclude each other; such places as the manor house of Chesney Wold are connected with a slum like Tom-all-Alone's by lines of pure coincidence and intrigue. This is one of the potential weaknesses of the manifold method. Plots insist on becoming idiosyncratic and produce several disparate stories rather than one multisided story. Aristotle required a "single effect" for any drama, and though that is too restrictive for novels, a general kind of unity is worth attempting.

Perhaps the most famous example of a novel with a split in its structure is Tolstoy's *War and Peace.* In his *The Craft of Fiction,* Percy Lubbock argues that there are two "stories" (and he uses the word approximately to mean "plot") which have only a coincidental relationship. One is the story of private people—Pierre, Natasha, Andrei, and their friends and families. The other is the drama of nations in conflict, with the Czar, Napoleon, Kutuzov, and other figures as the actors. The first is about the cycle of life from youth to age, while the second is about the clash of historic ambitions. Lubbock says:

> I can discover no angle at which the stories will appear to unite and merge into a single impression. Neither is subordinate to the other, and there is nothing above them (what more could there be?) to which they are

both related. Nor are they placed together to illustrate a contrast; nothing results from their juxtaposition. Only from time to time, upon no apparent principle and without a word of warning, one of them is dropped and the other resumed.

He adds that Tolstoy was trying, without knowing it, to write simultaneously an *Iliad*—which is a story of men—and an *Aeneid*—which is the story of a nation. This does not deny the greatness of *War and Peace,* but Lubbock suggests that it could have been even greater had Tolstoy recognized the incongruity in its form.

Vanity Fair is another case of two plots that have generally the same weight and that seem to balance each other off without having a great deal of connection. Thackeray had their paths cross now and then, notably in the Brussels scene before Waterloo when the Amelia Sedley plot and the Becky Sharp plot are thrown together under the same roof, but usually they remain independent. Independent—but balancing each other. This is the secret of why the book does not fall apart. Although it cannot be called truly unified, it does have a system of correspondences that prevents a fatal crack. The bold, scheming, shrewd and realistic Becky and the good, kind, womanly Amelia—the constantly implied comparative makes the two plots share a moral view.

Thus, the writer who wishes to use some scheme of double or multiple plot should carefully consider the dynamics—where the plots come together, how they reinforce each other or how they divide from each other, whether they have unconnected endings or endings that jointly contribute to whatever final meaning the book has. On one hand, they should be distinct enough so that they seem to be different explorations of actions and people; on the other hand, they should be congruent enough to belong in the same book.

William Faulkner once tried to alternate two contrasting stories in a novel called *The Wild Palms*, and the result is almost a textbook example of how not to yoke together by force a pair of incongruous plots. One concerns the love affair of a woman who has deserted her husband and children. Interspersed is the story of a convict who is freed by accident, has to survive a deluge, and finally returns voluntarily to prison.

The favorite Victorian multistrand plot has found its late twentieth-century employment with a capable generation of suspense writers (John Le Carré, Len Deighton, et al.). Shifting briskly from one place and set of characters to another scene of action and another set of characters and so on, they give an impression of complexity and diversity to what might otherwise seem a banal story. A good example of this is Frederick Forsyth's striking *The Day of the Jackal*. The method has been so thoroughly taken over, however, that serious novelists hesitate to use it lest their readers begin anticipating the appearance of the terrorist hit men or the CIA agent.

ECONOMY VERSUS DIGRESSION

Everybody remembers Chekhov's famous remark about plot: "If a shotgun hangs on the wall in the first act, it must go off in the last act." There is some ambiguity in that, but it is

usually taken to mean that a plot maker should not introduce
something unless he plans to use it. (Chekhov violated this
rule frequently and with much pleasure.) Some other expert
witnesses on the question ought to be called:

[Laurence Sterne:] Digressions . . . are the sunshine;
—they are the life and soul of reading! Take them out of
this book [*Tristram Shandy*] for instance,—you might as
well take the book along with them;—one cold eternal
winter would reign in every page of it; restore them to the
writer;—he steps forth like a bridegroom.[4]

[V. S. Pritchett:] What is it that attracts us to the
Russian novelists of the nineteenth century? . . . The real
attraction of that censored literature is its freedom—the
freedom from our kind of didacticism and our plots. The
characters of our novels, from Fielding to Forster, get up
in the morning, wash, dress, and then are drilled for their
roles. They are propelled to some practical issue in
morality, psychology or Fortune before the book is done.
In nineteenth century Russia . . . there is more room to
breathe, to let the will drift, and the disparate impulses
have their ancient solitary reign. . . . Turgenev, who knew
English literature well, used to say that he envied the
English novelists their power to make plots; but, of
course, he really disdained it. The surprises of life, the
sudden shudders of its skin, are fresher and more
astonishing than the imposed surprises of literary
convention or the teacher's lesson.[5]

[Fyodor Dostoyevski:] I can never control my material. Whenever I write a novel, I crowd it with a lot of separate stories and episodes; therefore, the whole lacks proportion and harmony . . . how frightfully I have always suffered from it, for I have always been aware it was so.[6]

[André Gide:] He [Paul Claudel] speaks . . . with the greatest scorn of English writers in general "who have never learned that the rule of 'nothing unessential' is the first condition of art."[7]

[Ernest Hemingway:] It wasn't by accident that the Gettysburg Address was so short. The laws of prose writing are as immutable as those of flight, of mathematics, of physics.[8]

But this collection of conflicting testimony is enough to confuse the wisest juror. An English novelist defends tangents and digressions; another English novelist says that his country's fiction has always been too regimented by plot and hails Russian freedom from it. A great Russian novelist says that his own work suffers from too many digressions and lack of discipline. A Frenchman says that the English novel is full of irrelevance. An American novelist says that economy is at the heart of good writing. The only one lacking is a Turkish critic to declare that they are all wrong and that the glory of the Turkish novel has been its ability to remain absolutely relevant to the plot while being delightfully irrelevant at the same time.

In fact, this is the answer—though not from Turkey. A

particularly lucid comment from Ford Madox Ford strikes the heart of the problem:

The first thing you have to consider when writing a novel is your story, and then your story—and then your story! . . . Any digression will make a *longueur*, a patch over which the mind will progress heavily. You may have the most wonderful scene from real life that you introduce into your book. But if it does not make your subject progress, it will divert the attention of the reader. A good novel needs all the attention the reader can give it. And then some more.

Of course, you must appear to digress. That is the art which conceals your Art. The reader, you should premise, will always dislike you and your book. He thinks it an insult that you dare claim his attention, and if lunch is announced or there is a ring at the bell he will welcome the digression. So you will provide him with what he thinks are digressions—with occasions on which he thinks he may let his attention relax. . . . But really not one single thread must ever escape your purpose.[9]

THE EFFECT OF THE PLOT ON FICTION

None of this helps very much to explain what plot is, in a larger sense, what it does for a fiction and to a fiction. Its long history of trial and error is the history of an attempt to organize the raw material of human experience into a causal pattern of beginning, middle, and end that does not waste anything in the telling. What are the advantages, finally, of this feat of craftsmanship? Does its expert use result in art, or does it result in artifice?

As such questions have a habit of doing, these revert to Aristotle. He put "action" first as the main business of drama, and "character" second. This is a philosophical distinction of great significance. Once we accept action as the primary thing, we have set ourselves on the road to plot. The next great principle is the organization of human action in a pattern of cause and effect. Once that has been done, the course is set and the development is inevitable. Character, the secondary consideration, has to fall into line; it can no longer evolve freely because it must answer the commands of the plot.

Actually, what we have here are two basic ways of looking at life. The Aristotelian way tells us that we cannot expect to look directly into human minds. The only reliable evidence we have about human life is the way people act and what they do. What a woman or man does impels another to do something else. The ambiguous feelings, the incidental thoughts, or the irrelevant impulses are of no great importance because they are not finally expressed in what the person commits herself or himself to in the way of a deed. Character is read in actions, and that is the only useful way to know it, according to this view.

This seems to be a realistic and convenient way of comprehending human life, and it is therefore very reassuring. But, beyond that, it opens the way to moral judgment. One of the things that plot leads most powerfully toward is a verdict on the people taking part. Even if the judgment is implicit, it is nevertheless there. The very idea of a denouement demands a sorting out of life; a plot cannot end without the assigning of values, without the identification of right and wrong. In an abstract way, this is what the denouement really is. "A writer without a sense of justice or injustice would be better off editing the yearbook of a school for exceptional children," Hemingway once said to George Plimpton.

Still, our novel has become older and wiser and more charitable about its world. It is subtler in making decisions about right and wrong, guilt and innocence. It recognizes that good people can do wrong in adverse circumstances, that there are varying outlooks on morality in different cultures, that institutions or systems can be villains more than people. Thus, plots in modern novels are likely to end in a far more discriminative and subtle assigning of values and identification of right and wrong. For instance, in a novel about a failed marriage (and there are many of these in the modern canon), there may be no moral accusation against either person—the breakdown might have come from different chemistries, different heritages, or different sources of satisfaction. Yet some marriages have succeeded even against those odds. Here, there must have been some inner fault, some important failure of sensibility or intelligence that the writer perceives as a "wrong" although one without a moral stigma.

The view opposite from Aristotle's is that the knowledge of human beings begins with a knowledge of character and thus literary art should begin there as well. Character is destiny. What a man is dictates what he does and, although his reactions are partly a response to the actions of others, there is always the element of individuality. Thus, fiction, if it is to have truth as art, cannot follow the scheme of an imposed plot. It must take character as its main subject; character, with all its ramifications and contradictions. The novelist knows the inner truths of his people and only then can he see what actions will proceed from them. Beginning from such premises, the author may also have accompanying moral ideas, but he does not let them restrict his final conclusions—his main search is for psychological truth. This is a very sketchy statement of a modern objection to plot. For the moment, it is well to return to the examination of how plot affects all the other elements of story.

A scheme based on action—as the dramatists were very quick to see—is a useful way of selecting what should be included and what should not be. And it gives plot makers a wonderful rule for economy. The idea of the three unities makes a good—but too doctrinaire—formula for that belief. "Nothing unessential." Every shotgun loaded to fire. All events a contribution to the royal scheme of action. And there is another thing—the plot-scheme is a great mobilizer as well. It makes other elements of the story do their duty. For instance, the notion of a setting as a landscape or cityscape that the author can paint in luxuriant detail just in order to surround us with an aura is ruled out. Places are functional. Characters keep appointments with the plot in some very specific locale, or else they appear in a setting so neutral that it is no more than a backdrop. Finally, there is a drive toward a precise style and the exact use of words.

The main issue is over the role of character. Laying aside for a moment the philosophical argument that stems from Heraclitus, it is possible to say that plot-scheme often is able to mobilize character in a brilliant way—even if purely for its own uses. As Frank O'Connor says: "Intrigue [i.e., plot] has the great advantage of enabling a novelist to make his characters show their paces, to submit them to a variety of tests and to develop them in unexpected ways. . . . Above all, intrigue imposes a standard of mere relevance, and saves the English novel from the atmosphere of utter irrelevance we so often find in Russian novels."

Plot has the remarkable capacity of compelling a fiction writer to show character positively. "Francis Macomber was a coward." "Jay Gatsby dreamed of recovering the past." These are passive statements. We have the author's word for it, but his word may or may not be true. In the midst of a plot, a character must act in order to prove himself/herself, in order to attain being.

Even so, plot probably never would have been so fascinating for authors had it been no more than a method of organizing material in an interesting way. It offers the writer a ready-made and efficient scheme for articulating his ideas. Right and wrong, blame and amnesty, punishment and reward, guilt and innocence, celebration and condemnation— these are all possibilities of the denouement. It is a kind of miniature Last Judgment in the small world of the fiction.

Critics note that something may go drastically wrong at this point. They note how often the traditional plot seems to go dead at the end. Young love is rewarded too regularly, ambition is punished too automatically; in fact, the most interesting speculations aroused in the early pages have received banal answers in the end. This always seems to happen when an author thoughtlessly accepts the conventional moral outlook of his time. Lacking any interesting or complicated moral perception of his own, he tells his readership—or his audience—what it thinks it already knows. His imagination may be lively enough to set things in motion but fail when it comes to consequences.

In an essay titled "Writing Short Stories," Flannery O'Connor tells this little tale:

> I have an aunt who thinks that nothing happens in a story unless somebody gets married or shot at the end of it. I wrote a story about a tramp who marries an old woman's idiot daughter in order to acquire the old woman's automobile. After the marriage, he takes the daughter off on a wedding trip in the automobile and abandons her in an eating place and drives on by himself. Now that is a complete story. There is nothing more relating to the mystery of that man's personality that could be shown through that particular dramatization. But I've never been able to convince my aunt that it's a complete story. She wants to know what happened to the idiot daughter after that.
>
> Not long ago that story was adapted for a television play, and the adapter, knowing his business, had the tramp have a change of heart and go back and pick up the idiot daughter and the two of them ride away, grinning madly. My aunt believes that the story is complete at last, but I have other sentiments about it.[10]

In her individual way, Flannery O'Connor is affirming the belief that the source of fiction is an author's conception of particular people—and that their actions are the outcomes of their personalities. That is significant when one remembers that the conception of the individual has grown immensely more complex, subtle, and extensive in the last hundred years. Plot, like a play director, demands that characters display themselves in just the actions that are functional. That demand could be accepted in an age that took a relatively simple view of human personality. In the work of Henry James and that of Fyodor Dostoyevski, to single out two great transitional novelists, that tyranny was no longer possible.

Both writers knew too much and felt too much about human psychology, the inner life, to be able to machine their characters into efficient functions of a plot. There were, of course, complex psychological portraits in literature before the mid-nineteenth century, but they were the exceptional work of a Shakespeare or a Stendhal.

The vast, gradual shift in the basic assumption of fiction came not so much through a boredom with stale plots and worn-out devices as through new ideas of how men and women can be known and understood. The "consistent" character who appears in plotted drama has no private life. Aristotle said, "Within the action, there should be nothing irrational. If the irrational cannot be excluded, it should be outside the scope of the tragedy." But the new assumption is that the irrational part of human life must be taken into account as fully as the logical. This led to a conception of the whole pattern of fiction that has been called "organic form" (discussed in chap. 9).

In the *Poetics,* one of Aristotle's chief examples for his demonstration of the workings of plot is Sophocles' tragedy *Oedipus Rex.* It serves admirably to illustrate the fate-and-action structure of the tale of the prince who would kill his father and marry his mother. It is a good plot in the classic sense. But, many years later, the inventor of psychoanalysis would look at the story again and see in its depths another, more primal plot. His conclusion was that the reason the ostensible plot aroused such feelings of terror and pity was that we were, without knowing it, responding to the secret plot that mirrors the submerged experience common to all of us.

PRACTICAL SUGGESTIONS—A CHECKLIST FOR PLOT AND STORY

It is not a bad idea for the beginning writer to follow traditional principles of construction in writing his first stories or novel. It gives him a reliable system of reference until he is quite confident of the departures he wants to make and the ways in which his originality will best operate. Here is a checklist of questions the author should be able to answer about his fiction.

1. What is the basic idea or subject of the story?
2. What is the chief question in the story? (*The Great Gatsby:* Will Gatsby get Daisy back again? *For Whom the Bell Tolls:* Will Robert Jordan successfully blow up the bridge?)
3. Who wants what? Most important, what is the protagonist's aim?
4. Why? (Motivations.)
5. Who or what stands in the way of this aim?

6. What plan does the protagonist make toward reaching his goal?

7. Will that produce countermeasures from his adversary? If there is no personal opponent, what does oppose the protagonist? E.g.: Forces of nature? His own faults? An institution or a system?

8. Is the struggle in the story an inner conflict? A person-to-person conflict? Both?

9. Is the action started by the principal character's want or by that of a secondary character?

10. Is a potentiality for conflict established early in the story?

11. Whom is the reader meant to "cheer for"?

12. The sympathetic character—what does he or she have at stake?

13. Does any character undergo a personality change? How? Why?

14. How well is the situation established at the beginning? Is the exposition brought out in terms of conflict and activity?

15. How does the author excite curiosity at the beginning and maintain suspense thereafter?

16. Does the story get in focus and stay there?—that is, meet the tests of unity, a strong protagonist, a clear objective?

17. Where is the point of attack in the story?—that is, where does the protagonist hit resistance as he drives toward his objective?

18. Are there some scenes that (a) begin with a disagreement, (b) develop the discussion, (c) arrive at a decision, and (d) produce an action? (Minor climax and resolution.)

19. Does the dialogue, by and large, develop and carry forward the story? Or is it just conversation?

20. Is each scene functional? Does each carry the story forward?
21. Does the story mount in tension?
22. Does it stay in key, maintain the same tone?
23. Are you (the reader) convinced of the inevitability of the situation?
24. Both at the beginning and thereafter, does the story place interesting people in juxtaposition to create a provocative situation?
25. Are the secondary characters detailed and defined or described, for example, as "Betty, a secretary, age twenty-six."
26. Does the climax dramatize and complete the author's intention in the story?

We must point out that these questions are not any sort of litmus test as to whether the novel or story will in the end prove to be an artistic success (though they can point the work in that direction). Nor is there a categorically "right" or "wrong" answer to most of the questions. The list is meant to stimulate the writer to reexamine what he has done and to recognize what he may have overlooked and what he has accomplished in the course of an outline or first draft. For example, question number 8 is a recognition question. It assumes that the author has established some sort of struggle or opposition in his story. (The only wrong answer would be to say that there is no conflict.) The writer then looks at this aspect of the story and, perhaps, decides that he has overemphasized the personality conflict between characters A and B at the expense of a demonstration of the inner conflict A is having concurrently.

Question 13 is another recognition question. It is meant to stimulate further question in the writer's mind: Character X, an unpleasant sort in the early going, has a couple of hard knocks that turn out to be learning experiences, and she begins to change for the better. Toward the end, she has become a sympathetic character. The writer—in response to the question—isolates that aspect of the story and tries to decide whether he has justified this change completely and has made the process convincing to the reader.

In general, if the answer to any question is "no," or "there is none," that would indicate a flaw in the plan for the story. If the answer is positive, the writer should ask himself how well he has carried out the obligation that the question implies. (E.g., question 12: Is it perfectly clear throughout that character Y is trying to preserve her integrity in situations where she could get quick advancement by bending the rules?)

Probably there is no short story to which all of these questions would apply—the writer has to use his selective judgment to choose those that do. Many more novels—assuming they follow some established plot-scheme—should furnish answers to most or all of the queries. The more satisfactory answers there are, the more successful the structure of the novel will prove to be.

Notes to Chapter 8

1. Angus Davidson, trans. (New York: Farrar, Straus & Cudahy, 1957), p. 44.
2. London: William Heinemann, 1949; pp. 254–55.
3. *Mirror in the Roadway* (New York: Alfred A. Knopf, 1956), p. 80.
4. *The Life and Opinions of Tristam Shandy, Gentleman* (New York: Clonmel Society, 1899), 1:118.
5. *The Living Novel* (New York: Harcourt, Brace & World, 1947), p. 216.
6. Edith Colbourn Mayne, trans., *The Letters of Fyodor Dostoevsky* (New York: Macmillan Co., 1914), p. 217.
7. Justin O'Brien, trans., *The Journals of André Gide* (New York: Alfred A. Knopf, 1947), 1:163.
8. *Ernest Hemingway: Selected Letters* (New York: Charles Scribner's Sons, 1963), p. 594.
9. *It Was the Nightingale* (Philadelphia: J. B. Lippincott Co., 1933), p. 211.
10. From *Mystery and Manners* (New York: Farrar, Straus & Giroux, 1968), pp. 94–95.

NINE

ORGANIC FORM
AND FINAL MEANING

A MILLION WINDOWS

It was quite like Henry James to think of fiction as the facade of a very large country house. Its vast expanse of front, he says, is pierced by a million windows of all shapes and sizes. Some are very broad—like picture windows, perhaps—some have balconies; some are narrow and slit-like, and some are low-browed. Inside at each of the windows is a watcher with a pair of unique field glasses, and no view through one set of binoculars is identical with that of any other. Everyone there is looking at the same landscape and the same human show, but some see more while others see less; one sees black in the places where his neighbor sees white; one sees big where another sees small; and one sees coarse where another sees fine. When a new watcher comes and opens a window that has always before been shuttered, there is no way of predicting what he will or will not behold from his unique vantage. This is James at his most expansive and tolerant.

Other images came to the minds of other writers when they thought about a definition for fiction. Stendhal saw a mirror carried along the roadway of life; Trollope saw a pulpit from which the author preached sermons; Richardson saw a "gilded pill," sweet outside and good medicine within; Matthew Arnold saw a pipeful of opium.

It seems that whenever a writer sets out to tell us what fiction is, he ends up by telling us instead what he thinks it ought to do—with the honorable exception of Henry James. It ought to reflect life, or it ought to be a beneficial lesson, or it ought to put us into a dream world. But all this confusion can be reduced to two fundamental philosophies about the art of fiction and its reason for being. The first stresses aim and the second stresses form.

As suggested in the previous chapter, there is a certain kind of writer who has a sense of mission, either abstract or specific, and that writer is destined to arrive at some moral evaluation of his slice of the world. Plot was invented for him; it is his supreme instrument through which to express a judgment of human actions. There is another kind of writer whose fictional strategy comes from a different psychology.

The belief in fiction as a form comes from this different psychology. The revolt against the reign of plot, which began in the late nineteenth century and continues today, puts forward two strong dissents. The first is against taking no more than the outward view of people—or, by his deeds alone shall ye know him. Instead, fiction must begin with the inward life of character, sensibility, psychology, thought, resources. The second great anti-thesis is against verdict-giving itself. This view holds that, although the writer should examine among other things the moral nature and moral behavior of mankind, he ought not to give up his credentials as an honest witness in order to sit on the judge's bench. As Chekhov said, it is for the artist to pose the great questions, not to decide on them, and the completely satisfying novel (or story) is one that sets all the problems correctly. Or, as D. H. Lawrence said, true morality in the novel is a balancing of things in the scales. When a novelist exerts his ideological prejudice, it is like putting a thumb on the scales to give false weight to one side.

Thus, the idea of a novel as a kind of natural form resulted in an entirely new development in fiction and, for a name, it borrowed a phrase from Coleridge's Shakespearean criticism. That name is "organic form." Coleridge made a distinction between form or discipline that is imposed on material (which includes the plot) and organic form. He said that organic form is "innate; it shapes as it develops itself from within, and the fullness of its development is one and the same with the perfection of its outward form." He thought of it as something like a force of nature that shapes a growing thing; in Shakespeare's plays, it was a conscious artistic skill directing "a power and an implicit wisdom deeper than consciousness."

In actual practice, it is largely an inheritance from the great Russian writers of the nineteenth century and their preference for a freedom in planning fiction. Careful structure was a hindrance; emotional leitmotif, as in music, was what they cared about. (There were exceptions—the fine short story writer Nikolai Leskov, for instance—and none of them threw plot entirely overboard.) The short story became far less a matter of what-happens-to-cause-something-else than a matter of watching some human situation develop in all its highlights and shadows. To take some examples, there is the idea of loving identification in Chekhov's "The Darling"; or of ingratitude in his "The Chorus Girl." In one sense, these are simple stories—they do not have an artful complexity of events. We look through clear windowpanes as we watch people in their emotional relationships. The best of Chekhov's stories are extremely fragile to the touch of criticism. They hang together and make a whole just by a sort of cobweb miracle of intersecting lines of meaning. They cannot be outlined and they should not be reduced to such bald descriptive phrases as used above. It is true that "The Chorus Girl" is about ingratitude, but that is only one facet of the story. It is also about natural generosity, about hypocrisy, false pride, insensitivity to others, shallowness, stupidity—and about a simple perplexity over all these things. Plotted short stories narrow toward the end and focus on their meaning. The Chekhovian story opens up into multiple meanings.

There is an old and somewhat unfair critical comparison between Maupassant, the most expert of French short story writers, and Chekhov. It is unfair because Maupassant, in a certain mood, could write stories (like "Hautot, Father and Son") that Chekhov would have been happy to sign. But, on the whole, it means to suggest that Maupassant was usually driving toward a single point—oftentimes ironical—while a Chekhovian story is always telling us that life is impure, even messy. Whatever happens, it says, may have something ridiculous, something touching, something contemptible, something chilling about it all at the same time. It has the strange power to clarify our feelings about the complexity of life without ever making it seem less complicated. About the people in one kind of story, we feel: they did certain things that led to a fated end. Of those in the other kind of story, we can say: some behaved badly and some behaved well in different proportions, but, in the end, we understand their humanity.

The lesson was absorbed by all the good American story writers of the first half of the century from Hemingway and Faulkner to Katherine Anne Porter and Eudora Welty, and the nondeterministic, nonjudgmental story has become the norm in our own times.

We can begin to understand what is meant by organic form in the novel by realizing that it has some affinities to both plot and story. Real life may have no ready-made plots, but it does have recurring patterns and forms. We are born, we mature, we grow old, we die. But, within that given form for human lives, there is a more specific cycle that most of us share. We go to school, we fall in love, we marry, have children, provide for their early lives, part from them as their cycle enters maturity. There is no mystery as to why most people have always preferred a story with a beginning, a middle, and an end. The pattern is copied from the human tale itself.

The classic novel in organic form is Tolstoy's *War and Peace* (leaving out the concurrent historical novel of Napoleon and the essays on history). It is an account of several people going through fifteen years of their lives, from youth to the approach of middle age. Their stories, which intersect, veer apart, then come close again throughout the novel, are ruled by two great sequences: the historical events of their time and the experience of growing up, falling in love, marrying, taking on the roles and responsibilities of their class. The historical cycle goes from peace to war to peace again with a deep effect on each private life. The personal cycle passes through youthful independence, then the emotional warfare and conflict of ideas in early womanhood or manhood, and finally arrives at the peaceful settlements of maturity.

Cause and effect play a part in the drama and, at certain points, so does chance. There is a sense of direction toward a destination, as in a plot. Yet, in *War and Peace*, their purpose is different from that in a plot-directed novel. They are not meant to unravel a secret or to combine for a denouement but are natural features of the roadway common to most of us in this life. This is not to say that Tolstoy had a deeper sense of existence than other great writers who used plot, but he had a greater ease about it. Those others had to spend a good deal of energy and skill in convincing us that their extraordinary versions of life do, in the end, have an acceptable fidelity to experience. He did not.

If plot is a courtroom trial with the evidence and the personae gradually revealed, conflicting testimony given, eloquence of defense and prosecution, a summing up, and a moral verdict of some kind, can its organic-form opposite have any moral nature at all?

One of the most striking short novels ever written in America is Saul Bellow's *Seize the Day*. The remarkable thing about it is that such a bleak novel—the consistent tenor is frustration and despair—should be such an often-read and -quoted one. It is probably Bellow's masterpiece in the shorter length, and it is developed in an organic way.

The story encompasses one day in the life of Tommy

Wilhelm, an unemployed salesman in his forties. During the course of the day, we see everything going wrong for him and we understand, little by little, what flaws there are in his character that have shaped his destiny. Tommy is not unintelligent nor is he insensitive, but he has never learned how to control his major collection of small weaknesses. Such a plan might have ended up as a minor, sarcastic comedy of a novel if told objectively, but Bellow has added the all-important, poignant factor of self-awareness. Tommy Wilhelm helplessly senses that he is inept, gullible, slack, greedy, wrongheaded, and self-deceptive, and we know this because the story is told mainly through his point of view. A fool and a loser is not at all the same as a man who is full of despair because he knows very well he is a fool and a loser.

Because he is almost without money, he goes to his father, Dr. Adler, who is prosperous and retired. Long ago, Tommy Wilhelm had symbolically rejected his father by taking on a new name. Now the doctor has no more love to give after all the years of watching Tommy's failures. He is world-weary and son-weary—and adamant against giving more money.

His next encounter is with Dr. Tamkin, who describes himself as a psychiatrist, but whose main occupation seems to be making small investments in the commodities market —he has taken the last of Tommy's money for an investment in lard. He is full of psychiatric jargon and inspirational advice and he is—as Tommy suspects but cannot quite discern—a thorough charlatan. A combination of wanting something for nothing and a subconscious acceptance of his role as a victim have drawn Tommy to the worst possible adviser.

The third encounter is a telephone blowup with Margaret, the wife from whom he is separated. It is, of course, over
money, but the basic quarrel is over faithlessness. Finally, in
a powerful last scene, Tommy wanders into a funeral parlor
and, overcome at the sight of the stranger in the coffin—who
could or should be Tommy Wilhelm—breaks into tears and
sobbing.

It would be hard to imagine a novel more filled with
moral questions, moral weaknesses, and moral paradoxes. A
man who is neither stupid nor vicious fails to make the
"honorable" but difficult choice at every turn in his life.
Others err through the inflexibility of their principles or
through hypocritical denial of principle. But, like any good
novel in organic form, it is a book of questioning rather than
solution giving, Socratic rather that Aristotelian. It fits Chekhov's demand to pose the great questions without answering
them.

In form, *Seize the Day* fits the organic strategy as well.
The whole story arises from Tommy Wilhelm's character, so
fully and vigorously imagined that its events and his associa-
tions with other people spring from it naturally.

The structure of *Seize the Day* is fairly simple, but other
modern novelists have found more complicated ones for organic fiction. Joyce's *Ulysses*, for example, is a novel of many
superimposed designs—the analogical connection with
Homer's *Odyssey* being only one of them. *Mrs. Dalloway* is
a rather elaborate pattern of crisscrossing time and space in
the several consciousnesses of the characters as they move
about London in the course of a day. D. H. Lawrence's two
connected novels, *The Rainbow* and *Women in Love*, are about

the problems of retaining individual freedom in contrast to or
in conflict with the sacrifice demands of any man-and-woman
union. All of these major modern novels involve values, but
always as the characters encounter choices along the way. No
novel of organic form is teleological, in the sense of being
directed toward a strictly definable end.

In an important work of modern criticism, *Axel's Castle*,
Edmund Wilson describes organic form in the novel from a
slightly different angle:

It [*Ulysses*] is an organism made up of "events,"
which may be taken as infinitely inclusive or infinitely
small and each of which involves all the others; and each
of these events is unique. Such a world cannot be
presented in terms of such artificial abstractions as have
been conventional in the past: solid institutions, groups,
individuals, which play the part of durable entities—or
even of solid psychological factors: dualisms of good and
evil, mind and matter, flesh and spirit, instinct and
reason; clear conflicts between passion and duty, between
conscience and interest. Not that these conceptions are left
out of Joyce's world: they are all there in the minds of the
characters and the realities they represent are there, too.
But everything is reduced to terms of events . . . which
make up a "continuum," but which may be taken as
infinitely small. Joyce has built out of these events a
picture, amazingly lifelike and living, of the everyday
world we know—and a picture which seems to allow us to
see into it, to follow its variations and intricacies, as we
have never been able to do before.[1]

SYMBOLISM

The barest definition of a symbol is "something that stands for something else." Along with this goes the idea of disproportion or disparity between the symbol and the thing symbolized. Something concrete will denote an abstract idea or cluster of ideas. A small thing represents a much larger thing; a part stands for the whole; one action symbolizes a whole complex of human attitudes.

There are perfectly conventional symbols with a long history. Among them, scales stand for justice, gold for wealth, white for purity, the cross for Christianity, and so on. Folkway symbols are such things as a cloverleaf for good luck, red hair for a fiery temper, or a fox for cunning. In literature, the most elaborate and systematic use of symbolism is Dante's *The Divine Comedy*, which is based on the established symbols of Christianity related in a system of logic.

The Symbolist movement of the nineteenth century introduced a radical concept of the symbol as a private and personal thing. Its meaning depended on the sensibility of the author rather than on any generally accepted meaning. Certain images were meant to suggest sensations in a quite subjective way, more often producing a mystery than a statement. Luckily, the movement is now embalmed in the history of French literature.

In fiction, three kinds of things can carry symbolical meanings: an object, an event, and a character. The all-important requirement is to keep the name tag invisible. A symbol should belong so naturally to the course of the story, to its furnishings or to the behavior of its inhabitants, that it cannot seem to be manufactured for the occasion or to spotlight some particular meaning.

It can be as simple as a man washing his hands. Usually quite a nonsymbolical act—but, in Dickens's *Great Expectations,* Mr. Jaggers, a lawyer, has a deep sense of guilt on his conscience and thus figurative dirt on the hands he is frequently trying to clean.

It can be as encompassing as the Swiss tuberculosis sanitarium in *The Magic Mountain,* which Thomas Mann made to stand for the sick and disordered society of all Europe. It can be as personal and pathological as Moby-Dick was for Captain Ahab. It can be as much of a foreboding omen as the eyes of Dr. T. J. Eckleburg—whose huge, disembodied orbs stare from a signboard over the dumping ground where Nick Carraway first meets Buchanan's mistress in *The Great Gatsby.*

There is an emphatic use of symbol in the short story "Three Million Yen" by the gifted contemporary Japanese writer Yukio Mishima. The story concerns a young couple called Kenzo and Kiyoko who are visiting an amusement park about fifty miles from Tokyo. This nice, middle-class pair are almost insanely prudent. They have budgeted far into the future, with their savings account divided into Plan A for a new washing machine, Plan B for a refrigerator, Plan C for a television set, and so on. A child is provided for under Plan X. "With their own plans so nicely formed, the two had nothing but contempt for the thoughtless, floundering ways of the poor."

Almost by chance, Kenzo buys three "million-yen crackers." These are large crackers with the baked-in design of a million-yen Japanese banknote. Kenzo bites into one and "a sweet, slightly bitter taste flowed into his mouth." They munch on the crackers slowly as they enjoy various concessions in the park. They go into a fantastic house called "Magicland" (something like what used to be called "the crazy house" in American amusement parks) and dream of having their own house: "Usually so prudent, they let their dreams run on this evening, perhaps, as Kiyoko said, because the million-yen crackers had gone to their heads."

Then comes a strange turn in the story. They walk into a coffee shop and meet an old woman who has been waiting for them. She is to take them off to a private house where the young couple will put on a "performance." The author never tells us what the performance was, but a number of clues strongly hint that it is a sex show (a fairly common form of entertainment in Japan).

Back at Asakusa Park later that evening, Kenzo and Kiyoko are in an irritable and disgusted mood. They have just made five thousand yen, but Kenzo says he would like to tear it up. Kiyoko persuades him to tear up the remaining million-yen cracker instead: "It was too large for one hand and so he took it in both and tried to break it. It was damp and soggy and the sweet surface stuck to his hands. The more it bent, the more it resisted. In the end, he couldn't break it."

Contrast this insistent, obvious, and rather crude symbolism with that of Balzac in one scene in *Père Goriot*. Half of the book is about Parisian society of fashion and wealth, and Eugène de Rastignac, the poor young man from the provinces, is trying desperately to make his way into that society. He has no idea how hollow and cruel it is; but Balzac, though he views it chiefly through Eugène's dazzled eyes, is always suggesting the reality.

The Vicomtesse de Beauséant, a distant relative of the young man, introduces him into the glittering world. He finds her kind and generous and, after her great love affair fails, even tragic.

As soon as her disaster is certain, she gives a great ball. She askes Eugène to recover her letters from her former lover, and, when he returns to her boudoir, she announces her departure to "bury herself in the depths of Normandy." In an agony of grief, she says that she wants to give Eugène some final token of her friendship because he is so noble and frank "in a world where such qualities are rare."

There is a moment of hesitation—it seems that Madame de Beauséant has not actually thought of these sentiments before and so she glances around the room hastily to find an appropriate present. "Ah, yes." Her eye falls on her glove box. It might seem difficult to make much of that, but the lady has considerable dramatic resources: "Here is the box I used to keep my gloves in. Every time I took them out before going to a ball or the theatre, I felt I was beautiful, because I was happy, and I never touched it without leaving some pleasant thought with it."

Thus far, the speech is plausible, even affecting. We breathe it in with Eugène. But then, in the last sentence, she falls into the chute: "There's a great deal of me in it, a whole Madame de Beauséant who no longer exists." Of course, we remember that the box is empty.

The symbol is a devastating comment on the vicomtesse and her life, but Balzac makes the symbol work in another ironical way. If Eugène is "good, noble, and frank," it is absurd to offer him a symbol of the vain life that has given her such unhappiness. But wait. It is just that vain and glittery life that Eugène wishes to have above anything else in the world. He will cherish the empty box.

Balzac's magic is astonishing. He has a lady who is trying to manufacture a symbol. But it turns out, in fact, to be a countersymbol against her and, in turn, a countersymbol against the man to whom she gives it. Few authors could achieve such a double sarcasm in one small glove box.

Both the Mishima and the Balzac examples are character-related. This kind of symbol is important because it denotes an important connection between a character and some abstract value (or supposed value). The beautiful lady thinks that she is giving up all the world, but she is giving up nothing. The lawyer is constantly asking for absolution from some godlike thing called Justice. In the best case, the force of these symbols flows back into the story and into our conception of the characters. But they are local symbols.

There is another class of symbol that seems to relate the whole fiction to some larger, and perhaps very involved, concept that stands outside the story. At the beginning of Joseph Conrad's *Heart of Darkness*, Marlow is on his way to the Congo:

> Once, I remember, we came upon a man-of-war anchored off the coast. There wasn't even a shed there and she was shelling the coast. It appears that the French had one of their wars going on thereabouts. . . . In the empty immensity of earth, sky, and water, there she was, incomprehensible, firing into a continent.[2]

It is, of course, a symbolic image of futility: Europe with her puny technology trying to subdue the immense, primeval heart of darkness.

This kind of outreaching symbolism often has to do with places. There is the previously mentioned magic mountain. There is the Mansfield Park of Jane Austen, a great house which can be said to represent in symbolic microcosm the life of the dominant class of her day. Evelyn Waugh's *Brideshead Revisited* is another microcosm of the same class 110 years later, in a changing world—and the stately home of Brideshead is its symbol.

This by no means exhausts the numbers of ways that symbols or symbolism can bear meanings in fiction. In practice, the important thing to remember is that symbols are not bright devices to be hung on the tree of the story. Nor can they be fabricated in an attempt to give the fiction an air of deep significance. They are serious and useful only when they are born from the narrative itself, when they come from the same well of imagination as the story.

The brief scene from Balzac is an example of how a natural turn in the story can be given a little symbolic stress, and this is the kind of effect that a writer in early practice should try for. The effect is slipped in; most readers would follow that passage without ever feeling that they had come face to face with a symbol. On the other hand, no intelligent reader could scan that scene without registering a deeper sense of Balzac's meaning than is apparent on the surface of the dialogue.

MEANING

Before we can begin to understand the ultimate meaning of any work of fiction, we have to consider:

1. Its general kind or category as a literary form.
2. Its more specific type or genre.
3. Its plan or structure as an aim toward meaning.
4. Its overall concept as a producer of meaning.

As for the first, some critics have detected, broadly, two types of fiction: romance and realism. Whatever names one might give them—imaginative fiction and naturalistic fiction, or the fabulous and the slice-of-life—they remain a division of two. The first is the heir of epic, myth, fairy tale, legend, ghost story. The second comes from recorded observation—true accounts, diaries, history, epistles, testimony.

General type tells us of general intentions. The more specific type or genre gives us a little better grasp. A satire and a utopian novel are both in the category of "romance," but each has a different end in view. Tragedies and comedies both have their traditional purposes. Then branching out are the numerous subspecies, such as the novel of manners, of romantic love, of adventure, of science fiction, of suspense, of ideas, and so on.

When we arrive at the overall concept as the producer of meaning, we have finally ruled out all the other novels in the world and have come to the thing that makes every piece of good fiction unique. To put it in old-fashioned terms, the concept is the soul, the spirit, the *Geist* of a novel or story. It cannot be captured outside the work itself. Of course, for purposes of criticism or the classroom, it has to be crudely summarized: "The futility of trying to recover the past"; "idealism, even though defeated once, lives on"; "You can't cheat an honest man." But this is a useful lie, as everyone knows. The concept generates story, and story produces emotions, and these emotions should culminate in that feeling too deep for words that comes just after reading the last sentence of a true fiction.

FALLACIES

On the negative side, there are some fallacies that often direct readers to wrong judgments about the meaning of a fiction.

The didactic fallacy is an evaluation by the moral intentions alone. If the sermon from the imaginary pulpit happens to agree with your own moral ideas, it is good. (But you did not notice that it is dull, contradictory, and badly expressed.) If contrary to your ideas, it is bad. (But you did not notice that it is brilliantly written.)

The historicist fallacy is that of judging a work by its relevance to its times. Thus, the novels of James Michener are important works because they contain so much information about the world while the novels of John Updike are unimportant because they do not deal with contemporary social issues.

The intentional fallacy is that of estimating a novel or story by what the critic (or reader) has decided to be the intention of the work. This is to brush aside any indication of meaning by the author himself and to delve into the author's supposed subconscious to find the real meanings.

The naturalistic fallacy is the judgment of fiction by its fidelity to facts alone. In fiction, actuality takes second place and changing the facts is only wrong when it leads to mistaken conclusions. Even the realistic novelist changes the world for his purposes.

The formalist fallacy is that of measuring the novel or short story in accordance with a supposedly correct form.

Somerset Maugham used to berate Chekhov because "his stories have no plot."

The fallacy of good taste is that of praising or condemning an author according to the reader's notions of what is agreeable or disagreeable. From Chaucer to Joyce to Norman Mailer, authors have been attacked for showing the "sordid" or "decadent" side of life. It is a fair subject for comment but not for arbitrary judgment.

None of these things need bother a writer as he sits down to start his piece of fiction—they are useless to think about at this point. But every writer who is in the course of learning his craft should beware of those traps of judgment.

HOW TO MAKE YOUR FICTION
HAVE AN ULTIMATE MEANING

Now you have arrived at the point where your sketchy map leaves off. Your guides, your equipment bearers, the other members of the climbing party have all stopped at various shelter points along the way. The peak of the mountain rises up in front of you. You are all alone. Your only comfort is the recollection that nobody ever reached the summit unless he went by himself.

Notes to Chapter 9

1. New York: Charles Scribner's Sons, 1931; p. 222.
2. *The Portable Conrad* (New York: Viking Press, 1957), p. 506.

SELECTED BIBLIOGRAPHY

Allen, Walter. *The Writer on His Art.* New York: McGraw-Hill Book Co., 1949.

Allott, Miriam. *Novelists on the Novel.* New York: Columbia University Press, 1949.

Borges, Jorge Luis. *Borges on Writing.* Edited by Norman Thomas di Giovanni, Daniel Halpern, and Frank MacShane. New York: E. P. Dutton, 1973.

Bowen, Elizabeth. *Collected Impressions.* New York: Alfred A. Knopf, 1950.

Cather, Willa. *On Writing: Critical Studies on Writing as an Art.* New York: Alfred A. Knopf, 1949.

Fitzgerald, F. Scott. *The Notebooks of F. Scott Fitzgerald.* Edited by Matthew J. Bruccoli. New York: Harcourt Brace Jovanovich, 1978.

Forster, E. M. *Aspects of the Novel.* New York: Harcourt, Brace & World, 1954.

Gardner, John. *The Art of Fiction.* New York: Alfred A. Knopf, 1984.

———. *On Moral Fiction.* New York: Basic Books, 1978.

Hemingway, Ernest. *Ernest Hemingway on Writing.* Edited by Larry W. Phillips. New York: Charles Scribner's Sons, 1984.

Hersey, John, ed. *The Writer's Craft.* Alfred A. Knopf, 1974.

Hills, Rust. *Writing in General and the Short Story in Particular.* Boston: Houghton Mifflin Co., 1977.

James, Henry. *The Art of Fiction.* New York: Charles Scribner's Sons, 1948.

———. *The Art of the Novel.* Oxford: Oxford University Press, 1947.

———. *The Notebooks of Henry James.* Oxford: Oxford University Press, 1947.

Lubbock, Percy. *The Craft of Fiction.* New York: Viking Press, 1957.

McCarthy, Mary. *On the Contrary.* New York: Farrar, Straus & Cudahy, 1961.

McCormack, Thomas, ed. *Afterwords: Novelists on Their Novels.* New York: Harper & Row, 1969.

O'Connor, Flannery. *Mystery and Manners.* New York: Farrar, Straus & Giroux, 1969.

O'Connor, Frank. *The Lonely Voice: A Study of the Short Story.* Cleveland: World Publishing Co., 1963.

———. *Mirror in the Roadway.* New York: Alfred A. Knopf, 1956.

Plimpton, George, ed. *Writers at Work: The Paris Review Interviews.* 4th and 5th ser. New York: Viking Press, 1967; 1981.

Pritchett, V.S. *The Living Novel and Later Appreciations.* New York: Random House, 1964.

Strunk, William, and White, E. B. *The Elements of Style.* New York: Macmillan Co., 1959.

Welty, Eudora. *The Eye of the Story.* New York: Random House, 1977.

Wharton, Edith. *The Writing of Fiction.* New York: Charles Scribner's Sons, 1925.

Woolf, Virginia. *A Writer's Diary.* New York: Harcourt, Brace & Co., 1954.

INDEX

CPSIA information can be obtained at www.ICGtesting.com
Printed in the USA
NW040439221212

894LV00002B/178/A

9 780312 051686